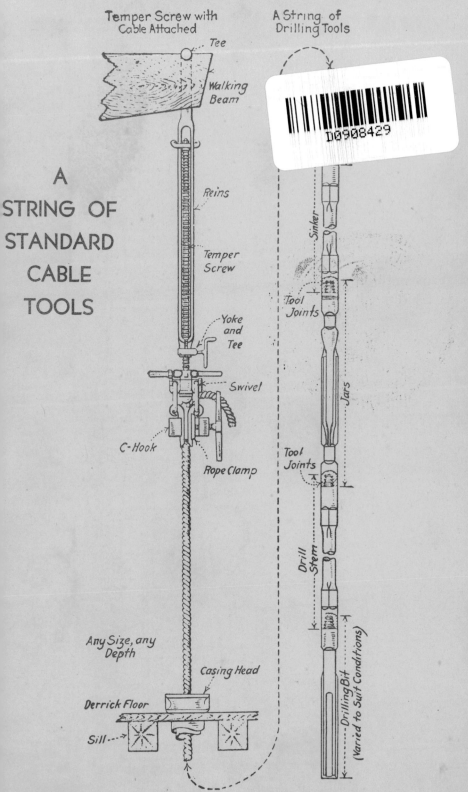

Temper Screw with Cable Attached

A String of Drilling Tools

Tee

Walking Beam

Reins

Temper Screw

Yoke and Tee

Swivel

C-Hook

Rope Clamp

Any Size, any Depth

Casing Head

Derrick Floor

Sill

Sinker

Tool Joints

Jars

Tool Joints

Drill Stem

Drilling Bit (Varied to Suit Conditions)

A STRING OF STANDARD CABLE TOOLS

From Dorsey Hager, *Oil Field Practice*, p. 47, courtesy McGraw-Hill Book Co.

350

762

TEXAS FOLK-LORE SOCIETY PUBLICATION

NUMBER XX

J. FRANK DOBIE, *General Editor*

Gilbert Morgan

Portrait of Gib Morgan in the
uniform of a Civil War Veteran

Gib Morgan

Minstrel of the Oil Fields

By

MODY C. BOATRIGHT

Illustrated By

BETTY BOATRIGHT

TEXAS FOLK-LORE SOCIETY
1945

PRINTED AT EL PASO
By CARL HERTZOG

CONTENTS

PREFACE

THIS IS THE FIRST PUBLICATION resulting from a study of the impact of the oil industry upon the folklore and the folkways of the American people. The study as a whole will have special reference to Texas, but there is a unity in the lore of oil that transcends state lines.

I have received grants in the aid from the Research Institute of the University of Texas and, through the Texas State Historical Association, from the Rockefeller Foundation. Librarians and archivists throughout the country have been universally generous. The National Archives and the Adjutant General's Office in Washington supplied me with records. The Carnegie Public Library of Pittsburgh made rare books and newspapers available to me, and Mr. William Scheide gave me access to the documents in the Drake Museum at Titusville. Mr. Moran of the *Oil City Derrick* had the files of that historic newspaper brought out of storage for my use.

Miss Edna Morgan, granddaughter of Gib Morgan, of Butler, Pennsylvania, has been most cooperative. Unfortunately fire destroyed her father's home and with it family letters and documents that would have been most valuable to me. Better than any documents, however, is Miss Morgan herself, who remembers the last years of her grandfather's life as well as a great deal of tradition about him handed down from her parents.

Mr. O. G. Lawson, of Cisco, Texas, not only told me the lore he had learned in West Virginia, but went to considerable trouble in finding and questioning other witnesses. Mr. R. B. Morris of Tionesta, Pennsylvania, former home of the Morgans, sent me tales and looked up information in local newspapers.

Scores of others have answered my letters and granted me interviews.

I have read extensively in the early history of the oil industry and in other fields related to this study. Written sources are, I believe, adequately indicated in the body of the book, and since oral sources are more important, I omit the customary bibliography.

I have not attempted to set down the tales verbatim as they were told to me. This would have necessitated the printing of each tale in several versions, would have made the book less interesting, and would have served no useful purpose.   MODY C. BOATRIGHT

The Life Gib Morgan Lived

GIB MORGAN AMONG THE HEROES

YEARS AGO IN THE OIL FIELDS OF West Texas I used to hear tall tales about a driller named Gib Morgan: how he built a vast hotel marvelously adapted to the southwestern climate in that every one of its hundreds of rooms had either an east or a south exposure; how he brought in a difficult well using a needle and thread for a cable and drill stem; how he had to shoot a bouncing tool dresser to keep the poor fellow from starving to death.

When I first heard these tales, I assumed that Gib Morgan was a synthetic hero of the cable-tool drillers—a creation of group imagination. But when I undertook the systematic collection of the folklore of the oil industry, I soon discovered that he was a man of flesh and blood: he had been born on a certain day and at a certain place; he had been a soldier and had fought in certain battles in a certain war; he had married; he had had children; he had worked in the oil fields of many states; he had retired and lived in homes for disabled veterans; he had died, leaving his tracks behind him. And before I had followed those tracks north through the Mid-Continent and Appalachian oil fields, back to his birthplace, which was also the birthplace of the oil industry, in Pennsylvania, I was convinced that I had found an American folk character of first importance.

What Paul Bunyan is to lumbering, what Pecos Bill is to the range cattle industry, what Mike Fink is to keelboating, Gib Morgan is to oil. More: he is both hero and poet, a scop who wore no man's livery, flattered no master, celebrated no deeds but his own. Both as a legendary character and as a man, he is much more vivid than these other figures, who are either outright creations of the folk mind or shadowy historical personages so surrounded by legend and so lacking in authentic documentation that their real personalities elude us. He is more like David Crockett, about whom has survived a large body of authenticated fact, another large body of popularly believed legend, and a third body of tall tales of the backwoods in which he reaches supernatural proportions.

Gib Morgan did not attain the stature of Crockett. He did not go to Congress or die in the Alamo. But he did create and disseminate an odyssey of comic folklore equal to the best in the Crockett Almanacs and superior to the best in the Paul Bunyan legend. This lore, richly imaginative and often satirical, is known in Texas, Oklahoma, Kansas, West Virginia, Pennsylvania—wherever oil is produced in the United States. It is known too, I am told, in Mexico, Venezuela, Russia, the East Indies—wherever American oil crews and technicians have gone.

Although Morgan's kinship with other American heroes of comic legend is plainly evident, he is in several respects unique. The characteristics of the type have been ably presented by Richard Dorson, who compares the legendary Crockett with the epic heroes of antiquity.[1] The hero delights in single combat with men and beasts; he is given to boasting; he takes pride in his weapons, his horse, his dogs, his woman; he has had a remarkable birth and has exhibited precocious strength in his childhood; in the end he meets a tragic death in which he is treacherously or supernaturally slain. It might be noted too that the heroes of American comic legend are for the most part notorious wasters of natural resources.

Gib Morgan does not exhibit all of these characteristics. One striking quality of his tales is the absence of supernaturalism. He was not a giant and made no pretense to the mastery of cosmic forces. This may be the result of the limitations he placed upon his imagination in making himself the hero of his tales. He was insistent upon this point. He had associates; and oil companies, notably Standard of New Jersey and Burmah Limited, figured in his narratives. But they were scrupulously kept subordinate. They were important only as stage settings and foils, only as instrumentalities through which he did his work. And since the hero was actually present in the flesh as narrator, present with his five feet, nine and a half inches of height and his hundred fifty pounds of weight, he could not be endowed with the size and strength attributed by the comic myth makers to Paul Bunyan and David Crockett. Morgan did, however, invent a giant tool dresser twenty-eight inches between the eyes and tall enough to grease the crown pulleys at the top of an oil derrick without taking a foot from the ground. But he was careful not to let Big Toolie steal his show. He made him a sort of good natured moron and eventually killed him off. So that although Tony Beaver, lumberman's hero of West Virginia took a day out of the calendar by stopping the rotation of the earth for twenty-four hours, and although Crockett, alarmed one day when the sun failed to rise, investigated and found the earth frozen on its axis, thawed it out and greased the axis with

[1] "David Crockett and the Heroic Age," *Southern Journal of Folklore*, VI, 95-102 (June, 1942).

bar's grease, Morgan never went for feats belonging more properly to demigods than to oil drillers.

Morgan's trade did not call for oxen, horses, guns, and the other paraphernalia of pioneer life. But he had grown up in western Pennsylvania at a time when game was abundant and horses important. The cycle of his tales shows Gib taking a day off now and then to make use of his long-range rifle, which shot salted bullets, his twenty-four-barrel fowling piece, and swift wolf hound. He had a remarkable horse twenty-two yards long with innumerable speeds forward and reverse, which served him well both on the road and on the race track.

Another striking characteristic of Gib Morgan's tales is their concern for conservation. The folk hero of the backwoods gloried in the destruction of game. The lumberman regarded it his duty to turn the forests into wastelands in the least time possible. It is a matter of historical fact that the pioneer oil industry was as wasteful as any. Not only was the recovery of underground oil inefficient, but gas was allowed to escape into the air, oil was permitted to flow into creeks killing fish and ruining land; and it was not unusual to open a casing head and allow a gusher to spout as a spectacle to entertain the public or to induce them to invest in the oil stocks. Gib Morgan was ahead of his time. He did not boast of gushers which sprayed the moon; he boasted of those he brought in and capped without spilling a drop.

Nor do Morgan's tales glorify fighting. He was not a boasting rip-snorter, half horse half alligator, a wolf with a barbed wire tail. In the cycle of his yarns there is only one account of a physical combat. It is burlesque of a high order, the story of a fight to end all fights.

The Morgan of the tales is not a wholly consistent character. Sometimes he does not appear any too bright; sometimes he is merely the witness of a strange wonder. But most of the time the trait chiefly emphasized is ingenuity. He is confronted with a difficult technical problem. After due meditation and perhaps some trial and error, he hits upon a solution so simple that he wonders that he has not thought of it before.

Not all of Gib Morgan's tales were original. Some of them have no relation to the oil industry and were traditional in the western Pennsylvania in which he grew up. These concern chiefly hunting and fishing and planting. One, the story of the bears eating the horses, is clearly an adaptation from Munchausen. Others,

4

like those of the bouncing tool dresser, involve common motives, although I suspect Morgan's tale antedates its analogues, for he was a driller when rubber boots made their first appearance in the oil fields. Gib Morgan did not create his tales from nothing. But when due allowance has been made for borrowing and adaptation, he remains the most fertile creator of comic folk tales known to America.

In spite of the excellence and wide distribution of his tales, Morgan, the hero of them, is hardly known except among a generation of oil workers becoming fewer each year. One reason for this fact is his chronological position. The Bunyan legend has been in the making since some of Paul's exploits got into print in a booklet printed as advertising by the Red River Lumber Company in 1914. Writers were soon on Bunyan's trail and by the middle twenties he was known all over America. Scholars soon afterwards unearthed the Crockett Almanacs published between 1830 and 1860 and brought the Crockett of comic legend to the attention of the public. Walter Blair and Franklin Meine have combed libraries for the legends of Mike Fink. Gib Morgan came between the periods most assiduously worked by the folklorists. He was already known among oil field workers as the Munchausen of the oil fields in 1880. His fame reached its height about 1909. This period has been comparatively neglected by those who have been searching for native American folk humor. Despite its tremendous social and economic significance, the oil industry has not appealed to the popular imagination as lumbering, mining, pioneering and cattle raising have. Drilling an oil well, even a gusher, has seemed less spectacular than felling a forest, fighting a panther with a butcher knife, or turning a stampeding herd of cattle.

As Gib Morgan's fame declined he was in many places supplanted by Paul Bunyan. Most cable-tool drillers who were active before the first World War can tell you about Gib Morgan. Most younger ones cannot. But they will tell you tales that Gib Morgan told and will attribute his exploits to Paul Bunyan. This process of substitution, in which one hero gets the edge on another and gradually displaces him, is familiar to every folklorist. And the reasons for Bunyan's edge are fairly obvious. Lumber is more widely distributed than oil, and therefore the lumber hero is more widely known. In addition, Bunyan had excellent press agents in Esther Shephard and James Stevens, and in the 1920's young book-reading oil workers, especially college men during summer vacation, carried his name into the oil patches in which they worked. Paul Bunyan had not long been before the public when journalists, feeling the need for some American superlative, made his name a common adjective. Thus an unusually large electric motor is referred to as a Paul Bunyan motor and a task requiring great strength or effort is called a Paul Bunyan job.

Gib Morgan has not become a household word. But any cable-tool driller who learned his trade in Pennsylvania, West Virginia or Ohio before the first World War knows that after all Paul Bunyan is a mere lumberjack who has never been near an oil well and who wouldn't know a Samson post from a headache post if he had. The real hero of the oil fields is Gib Morgan.

Gib Morgan's tales, however, transcend the oil industry. Created at a time when a resource hitherto unutilized and scarcely known was being spectacularly exploited, they symbolize the whole era of expanding geographical and industrial frontiers, the era of manifest destiny and spread-eagle oratory, the era in which the folk artists, as distinguished from the literary artists, in response to a deep social urge attempted to create a literature commensurate with the events of the times.

WHERE GIB MORGAN WAS BORN
AND HOW HE GREW UP

 THE FOLK HERO OF THE OIL FIELDS goes by several names: Gib Morgan, Gid Morgan, and sometimes Gil Morgan. The name that his parents wrote in the family Bible was *Gilbert*. This is the way his name appears in the public archives, and I have not seen his signature written any other way. Gilbert in family circles was shortened to *Gib,* and by this name he is still called by his surviving relatives and intimate friends. This too is the name most often in print during his lifetime and the one most generally associated with his tales. His biographer should use no other.

Gib Morgan's birth preceded the birth of the oil industry by less than eighteen years, only time enough for him to grow into an observant and eager youth. His birthplace was the village of Callensburg, Clarion county, in Western Pennsylvania, the date

6

July 14, 1842. He was one of a large family of children belonging to George Morgan and Elizabeth Shoup Morgan. Born six years after the marriage of his parents, he came near the middle of the group of eight who survived infancy. Both his parents were natives of Pennsylvania, his father having been born in Callensburg in 1815, and his mother in Allentown in 1817. She was still a small girl when her parents took her west and settled near the Morgans in what later became Clarion county. After their marriage in 1836 George and Elizabeth Morgan lived at Callensburg and at Alum Rock, an even smaller village nearby, until 1848, when they moved across the line to Emlenton, in Venango county. While living in Clarion county George Morgan made his living chiefly by farming, although he may have supplemented his income by lumbering and rafting. But as early as 1839 he had become a builder. There still stands in Emlenton a house said to have been built by him in that year. It is a substantial wooden structure in excellent repair. It is now a residence, but at one time it was the chief hotel of the village and was widely known during oil boom times as the Valley House.

George Morgan's object in moving to Emlenton in 1848 was not, however, to build houses. He erected a barge works on the Allegheny river at the mouth of Ritchey Run and there built the hulks from native timber and floated them downstream to Pittsburgh, where sides and other necessary fittings were added. The barges were then put into service transporting an increasing traffic in ore, coal, and lumber.

Emlenton was his residence for twenty years. In 1868 he established a barge works at Tionesta, in Forest county. This move was probably the result of a shift in the river traffic. Between 1859 and 1868 the oil industry had developed, first along Oil creek, which flows into the Allegheny at Oil City, about twenty miles above Emlenton, then around Franklin between Emlenton and Oil City, then up the river at Tidioute, and at Pleasantville, between Pithole creek and Oil creek. Production jumped from 2,000 barrels in 1859 to 4,800,000 barrels in 1869. By 1868 a crisis in transportation had been reached. Barges were more urgently needed than ever before, and Tionesta, near Tidioute and above the mouth of Oil creek, was a favorable location in which to build them.

George Morgan was soon to make another business venture. The first announcement of the new location of his barge works appears in the Forest *Press*, Tionesta, for March 6, 1868. On June 3 he announces that he "has leased the Greene and Gordon Mill on

Tionesta [creek] and removed his family to that place, where he will begin the manufacture of lumber. The old dam is gone [the announcement continues] but a temporary one has been erected and when the water falls sufficiently a permanent dam will be built."

The mill was at the mouth of Bear creek, and George and Elizabeth Morgan lived in the community by that name for six years. They then moved back to Tionesta, where they bought a house, still standing, on Vine Street. There George Morgan died in June, 1882. He never became wealthy. A newspaper report of 1872 tells of Harrison Morgan's losing a finger in the sawmill, indicating that members of the family worked at the mill.

George Morgan, however, was regarded as a successful business man. In the February preceding his death he was elected burgess of Tionesta "without opposition," and, to quote from his obituary in the Forest county *Republican*, "gave the affairs of the Borough his careful attention and bade fair to become the most useful officer the town has had for many years."

Gib Morgan sprang from a sturdy and respected sire.

It is a significant fact that the environment in which he grew up was essentially a frontier environment. The counties of western Pennsylvania before the coming of oil were sparsely populated. They had been off the beaten path of westward migration. Several routes from the eastern coast converged at Pittsburgh. That city once reached, few families cared to work their way up stream when they could easily put their belongings on a raft and float down the Ohio. Then too, the chief market for their products, once they were settled, would be New Orleans, and they naturally preferred lands nearer that market. Consequently Ohio and Kentucky settled earlier and more rapidly than western Pennsylvania. Another deterrent to settlement after Wayne's victory at Fallen Timbers in 1795 was confusion about land titles. Settlers who came into the region to acquire land often found themselves in litigation with large land companies, several of which had been organized to operate under the act of 1792, but which, the state contended, had not complied with the terms of the act. A test case reached the Supreme Court of the United States in 1805, which upheld the claims of the Holland Land Company against the settlers. Private claims were involved too. The first settlers in Clarion county came in 1801 and 1802 and settled on what they thought was vacant land. They afterwards had to purchase it from the Bingham estate.

Most of the western counties were created out of Allegheny

county by a legislative act of 1800. But many of them were paper creations only, and remained unorganized for three or more years. Warren county did not organize until 1801. Clarion, Gib Morgan's native county, was not created until 1839 and did not organize until 1840. Its population that year was less than ten thousand. Venango county, where he moved at the age of five, was organized in 1805. Its population in 1840 was 17,900.

But there were more people in the region than its economy could well support. Much of the land was poor and the farms were remote from markets. In a book published in 1865 Edmund Morris wrote:

> "Ten years ago a traveller passing through the country drained by Oil Creek, in Venango county, Pennsylvania, would have found most of it a barren, uninviting region, in many places very sparsely settled, and most of the settlers hardly able to gain a livlihood. . . . Money was a scarce commodity. . . . Men who in that day and region were rated well-off, comparatively, in the world's goods, rarely handled more than five hundred dollars in a year—indeed, he was esteemed a fortunate man who handled half that amount."

Similar testimony comes from J. J. McLaurin:

> "Scratching the barren hills for a meager corn crop, hunting rabbits on Sundays, rafting in the spring and fall, and teaming while the snow lasted barely sufficed to keep the gaunt wolf of hunger from the door of many a hardy Oil Creek settler."

Although the industrial population was insufficient to absorb what surplus the farmer had to sell, there were some industries. Steel was already important in Pittsburgh, which in 1840 had a population of 38,931. There were salt works in various places north of the city, coal and iron mines, and many small furnaces, some of them still using charcoal. There were lumber mills, but if Colonel Drake is to be trusted, the people derived little benefit from them.

> "They converted the lumber into cash," he wrote, "but very little of that cash ever found its way into the pockets of the inhabitants of Titusville and vicinity, as one man told me he had worked for them [Brewer, Watson, and Company] for fifteen years steady at $1. per day, and only received in that

time $21.50 in cash. The balance of his earnings he had received in goods from the store of company, and those at such high prices that he was then in debt to the company nearly $300. I merely mention this particular case to show that although the lumber company was becoming rich, the inhabitants were becoming poorer every year. One of the firm told me at that time that he knew just how many pine trees the company owned and about how much lumber they would make, and that it would take about five years to cut up the logs and run the lumber to Pittsburgh, and said, 'We shall leave here and the place will die a natural death. There will be no business. The people will have to starve or move, and in ten years the main street will be grown to grass.' "

Hemlock bark as well as lumber went out of the forests. Besides tanneries around Philadelphia there were large works at Wilcox in Elk county which processed nearly a million buffalo hides between 1845 and 1885. But the men who stripped the bark from the trees, living in miserable huts in the woods, were, even more than the lumber workers, symbols of poverty and squalor. In the folklore of the region their position was analagous to that of the squatter in Arkansas or the turpentine gatherer in Georgia.

One anecdote ran like this: An oil scout, sent to spy on a wildcat well up in the hills, took board and lodging in a bark peeler's hut. As he watched the woman cooking breakfast the next morning, he saw a mangy-looking cat asleep on the shelf above the stove. Not long after he had entered, the cat woke up, yawned, staggered around the shelf, lost its balance and fell into a crock of buckwheat batter. The woman grabbed it, wiped off the batter, and put it back on the shelf.

"I declare," she said, "that's two times you've fell into the batter this morning. If you fall in again, it won't be fitten to use."

In their poverty and isolation the people possessed a rich folklore. They sang doleful ballads about Lord Randall and Lord Lovell, and less doleful ones about Robin Hood. If they did not read to their children, they told them stories about Jack the Giant Killer and passed on to them a large body of tradition about George Washington and Half King at Fort Venango, about the Whisky Insurrection, about Indian massacres and captivities. George Morgan learned this lore as a child, and he transmitted it to his children, for he liked to talk about old times. It was said of him that "his reminiscences of early days told in his quaint way, made him a very companionable and agreeable guest."

Some of George Morgan's reminiscences must have been about hunting. In his youth men were still living who had shot buffalo in Pennsylvania. In Gib Morgan's own boyhood other game abounded. Passenger pigeons still nested along Tionesta creek. There were bear in the forests, and in spite of a state bounty of twenty-five dollars, timber wolves remained until about 1870. There were occasional panthers, and wildcat were numerous enough to give the oil industry a picturesque term. Naturally much of the folklore of the region concerned hunting. Here were found the tall tales about the prowess and lucky shots of the hunter so characteristic of rural America. A nimrod shoots a bear. The bullet goes through the bear and kills a buck some distance away. Then it ricochets and kills any number of turkeys lined up on a limb. The recoil of the gun kicks the hunter backwards. As he falls, a button from his pants flies off and kills a rabbit. He is knocked into the creek and comes out with his pockets full of fish.

One traditional tale that Gib used to tell in the first person concerned a city slicker's first visit to the country. As this man was walking along a hillside road one day, he met a farmer going to town with a wagon load of pumpkins. As the city man had never seen a pumpkin before, he stopped the driver to ask what they were. The farmer, instantly sizing him up for what he was, told him that they were mule eggs and talked him into buying one at five dollars.

The city man started walking down the road carrying his pumpkin under his arm. He had not gone far when he dropped it, and it went rolling down the hill. It gathered momentum until it burst to pieces on a boulder, near which a bush grew. Out of the bush jumped a rabbit. As the rabbit loped away, the city slicker called, "Here, colty, here. Here's your mammy."

There were stories too, ironic stories, about the fertility of the soil. The reason the pumpkins and the melons were so poor was that the fast-growing vines ruined them by dragging them around.

Gib Morgan grew up amid a body of folklore rich in tragedy, pathos and humor, especially the humor of exaggeration.

The tradition of letters was less evident. Travelers to the region have commented upon the ignorance of the isolated people.

" 'Content to live, to propagate and die,' " [wrote J. J. McLaurin] "their requirements and their resources were alike scanty. They knew nothing of the artificial necessities and extravagances of fashionable life. To most of them the great busy, plodding world was a sealed book, which they had neither the means nor the inclination to unclasp. The world reciprocated by wagging in its customary groove, blissfully unconscious of the settlers on the Allegheny's tributary. A trip on a raft to Pittsburgh, with the privilege of walking back, was the limit of their journeyings from the hills and rocks of Venango. Hunting, fishing, and hauling saw logs in winter aided in replenishing the domestic larder."

The people of Clarion county were considered even more ignorant than those of Venango. There the proportion of "original settlers was higher, many of them Dutch." The Turkey City farmer who refused to lease his land for a one-fourth royalty, but held out for one-eighth was not less skilled in arithmetic than many of his neighbors. Ida Tarbell reported that it was not unusual for "a Clarion county farmer, if offered an eighth royalty, to refuse it on the ground that it was too little, and to ask a tenth." The Oil Producers' Union felt that the non-cooperation of the Clarion county owners, too ignorant to understand the issue involved, was an important cause of the Union's defeat in its struggle with Standard Oil in 1872.

The state had, however, made an effort to establish schools in the outlying regions. The act of 1854 empowered townships to raise their common schools to high schools if and when local revenue was sufficient, but as late as 1860 there were ten or twelve townships without high schools. There were numerous private and denominational "academies," including one at Franklin and one at Clarion, but they were beyond the reach of the poor.

Yet a generation earlier George Morgan had somehow acquired a fair education. At Tionesta he was known as "a great reader [who] kept himself posted on the current affairs of the day." How much formal schooling he had I do not know. How much he was able to give his children I do not know. Gib must have gone through the common school at Emlenton, and he may have gone to a high school or an academy. At any rate he had a better education than most Venango boys of his generation. It is evident from certain legends about him that he was later regarded by his fellow

12

oil field workers as an educated man. One of these legends is that he was educated for the bar and that he had found the practice of law dull and had abandoned it for the more congenial life of an oil driller. He may have read law in some practitioner's office, but local tradition thinks not, and is unanimous in denying that he ever practiced. It is certain that he did not unless he did it before he was twenty. Another legend is that he was once a newspaper editor, "or at least a reporter," and, following the folklore of American journalism, that he was fired for drunkenness. At one time his tales and sayings used to be quoted in the press of the oil region, but I find no evidence that he was ever on the pay roll of a newspaper. A third legend which indicates that he was a man of some literary attainments beyond those of the typical oil worker of his day is that he was the author of a book. I shall return to this subject later, noting here that the specimens of his writing that I have seen exhibit a familiarity with the newspaper humor of his day, and employ the vocabulary of a man who has read.

Gib Morgan had just turned seventeen and was living at Emlenton, less than forty miles from Titusville when, on August 28, 1859, Drake's driller, Uncle Billy Smith, sent his son running to Upper Mill with the news that he had struck oil. The mill shut down and the workers rushed to the well to see Uncle Billy drawing oil with a bucket he had improvised from a piece of tin gutter pipe. The news soon reached Titusville and more people came. It reached Lower Mill and others came. It travelled down Oil creek to Cornplanter, soon to be rechristened Oil City, and more came. Down the Allegheny to Franklin and on to Emlenton it went, and still others came. Eventually, on September 13, it was published in the New York *Tribune* and thus reached the outside world.

Other derricks went up along Oil Creek, and down at Franklin at the mouth of French Creek, James Evans the blacksmith got busy. He bought some iron and second-hand pipe on credit, made a string of tools in his own shop, deepened his water well and got oil. Judge John S. McCalmont (later colonel commanding the Tenth Reserve Infantry) recessed court, and judge and jury, lawyers and litigants rushed out to Evans's place. A doctor arrived without hat, coat, or shoes. "Babies cried, children screamed, and two horses ran away." That night the constable called on Anna Evans, as he had been doing frequently of late. "I don't have to marry you now," she told him; "Dad's struck ile." "Dad's struck ile" became a by-word throughout the oil regions. It was used as a

13

refrain in two popular songs published in 1865. It reached the press and was copied by a London newspaper. A Pittsburgh capitalist offered Evans fifty thousand dollars for the well. "This is my well," said the blacksmith. "If you want a well, go dig your own."

But the first excitement was mainly local. It was not until the following summer that the influx of people from the outside began. In June, 1860, Thomas A. Gale wrote:

"The capitalists, as well as that large class not so rich as ready to venture, are streaming in from all quarters. Here, too, are men who have toughened their constitutions in the coal-beds of Ohio, the lead mines of Galena, and the gold placers of California. They barter prices in claims, and shares; buy and sell sites and report depth, show, or yield of wells, etc. etc. Those who leave today tell others of the well they saw yielding 50 barrels of pure oil a day. . . . The story sends back more tomorrow who must see before they can credit. . . . Never was a hive of bees in time of swarming more astir, or making a greater buzz."

Drake wrote James M. Townsend in August that the region was full of "anxious seekers all determined to make a fortune or burst in the attempt."

Oil had brought new faces, new characters to the quiet valley. It also brought tragedy. On April 17, 1861, a driller on the John Buchanan farm struck a pocket of gas. The well gushed in with an estimated initial flow of three thousand barrels. Soon a crowd gathered. There was an explosion and an acre of oil was in flames. Nineteen persons burned to death. Among them was Henry Rouse, whose fortitude has made him legendary character. He was standing about twenty feet from the well when the explosion occurred. As he ran he stumbled, rose and stumbled again. He was dragged from the flames mortally burned. During the five hours that he lived he dictated his will, leaving a considerable part of his fortune to the commissioners of Warren county for civic improvements and poor relief.

Equally impressive to the spectators, but for a different reason, was the death of another victim. "One poor wretch," says an eye-witness, "struggled out of the fire, believing himself in the hands of the evil one. His charred and naked body was speedily placed in a blanket, and he was borne from the place. He lamented his supposed arrival in [hell], in piercing tones of agony, which proceeded from lips burned to a cinder. . . . He moaned his own fate, and calling the names of various friends warned them of his own terrible punishment. Death ensued in four hours."

When Gib Morgan first saw an oil well I do not know, but he along with the other villagers must have journeyed up the valley to look at Drake's wonder. Nor do I know what he thought as he looked at it. If he saw in it the birth of an industry that would revolutionize the arts of peace and war; if he foresaw the automobile, the Diesel engine, the tractor, the airplane, the tank, he was gifted with keener insight than his elders and betters were. But he must have sensed as did his neighbors, that something important was happening, must have been stirred by the human drama that had come to his hitherto isolated valley, must have laughed at Anna Evans's dismissal of her lover, must have admired the heroism of Henry Rouse, and been shocked by the agony of the man who thought he was in hell. Perhaps even then he wanted to be a part of this new drama.

But before he reached man's estate, a call had come that he regarded more urgent than the call of the oil field. In heeding this more imperative call, however, he was unwittingly preparing himself for the role he was later to play as the minstrel of the oil industry.

HOW GIB MORGAN BECAME THE MINSTREL OF HIS REGIMENT

FORT SUMTER WAS FIRED UPON ON April 12, 1861. On April 13 Governor Curtin addressed the Pennsylvania legislature assembled in extraordinary session to consider the implications of this event. Said the governor:

"The insurrection must be met by force of arms, ... and a quarter of a million of Pennsylvania's sons will answer the call to arms, if need be, to wrest us from the reign of anarchy and plunder and secure for themselves and their children for ages to come, the perpetuity of the government and its beneficient institutions."

He made other speeches and issued proclamations in the same tone until his oratory filled the state.

On April 25, Gib Morgan, not yet twenty years old, went over to Franklin, the county seat, and signed his name as private in Company C, Tenth Pennsylvania Reserve Infantry. Since minors were not being accepted, he put his age down as twenty-one, and thus told, so far as I have been able to determine, the only lie he ever told for the purpose of deceiving.

When he had signed the roster of Company C, Gib thought he was in the army. He soon discovered his mistake. He and the other reservists were to encounter a long period of confusion and delay before they were permitted to serve under the Stars and Stripes—a period that was to have important consequences for Gib. The governor's eloquence had been too effective. So many young men had done what young Morgan had done that the state's quota, although raised from fourteen regiments to twenty-five, was full, and Secretary of War Cameron refused to muster in the other thousands who were clamoring to save the Union. At the same time he authorized certain individuals to raise companies and regiments.

Sharp messages were exchanged between Harrisburg and Washington. Governor Curtin asked Secretary Cameron to define his policy "so that the ardor of the people of this State should not again be cooled by changes." If the new militia could not be mustered into the United States Army, could they be equipped by the Federal Government? The Federal Army, he learned, could not furnish camp equipment, but the Secretary recommended that "your state do so, and present bill for same; clothing," the message continued, "is sometimes issued to volunteers, but at present we have not supplies for that purpose." And so it went. Governor Curtin ordered the reserve regiments to camps to train for three months unless they should be called into the national service before the expiration of that period.

Although uniforms from the Federal government were not forthcoming, the people of Venango county were not going to let their Company C go to camp looking like civilians. They passed the hat and took in nearly a thousand dollars. They bought good quality cloth at the woolen mills at Kennerdall, and the women of Franklin tailored it into uniforms. Decked out in their new clothes, Company C was christened the Venango Greys. They had kept their organization intact through May, and on June 6 they left by keel-boat for Camp Wilkins, near Pittsburgh.

Here the formal organization of the regiment was effected, and

16

the Venango boys had the satisfaction of seeing their own Judge McCalmont, a West Point graduate, elected Colonel. But there was little else to give them satisfaction.

A Philadelphia journalist reported that it was said at the beginning of the war that the oil region would turn out the best soldiers because here the men were used to drilling. He did not say who originated this pun, but it seems to have expressed an attitude quite typical of the boys from Venango. They had grown up hunting rabbits if not larger game; they felt that they already knew how to shoot as well as the next man; they were ready for battle. There were complaints about the food. The site of Camp Wilkins had been poorly chosen and sanitation had been neglected. "The Camp," says the official historian of the Pennsylvania Volunteers, "was in a filthy condition, and much sickness prevailed." Hospital facilities were inadequate.

A recruit from another regiment wrote home:

"My health is tolerably good. I have been sick with a severe cold one day so I could not drill, but a wet towel cured that and I had a turn of sick headache; beyond that I have been very well. I feel very well this morning. I had a good breakfast, had milk in my coffee, and last night we had butter.

"The day I had sick headache I got nothing for breakfast but a piece of dry bread, and at noon we had rice soup that was burnt so as to be nauseous. I ate a good quantity, however, and, consequently, unate it and ate no more till the next night."

On July 1 the Tenth moved up the Allegheny river twelve miles to Camp Wright. Here health improved, but because of the uncertainty of their status, morale continued to degenerate. A young man from the Erie Regiment wrote home to his father:

"We have been told by some officers that 'we were accepted; we were going to Chambersburg; we are not accepted; we are accepted for three years; those who would not enlist for the war would be sent home; they would be kept here until their three months expires; that companies A, B, C, F, and I only, would go for the war, and the rest would be disbanded,' and within ten minutes Major Schlaudecker had told me 'that none of the companies would go; that we would all go together, one way or the other.'

"Acting on the statement that our Company [K] would not

17

go, I went this morning and put my name on Company B's roll of war. Our captain said 'No man should leave his company till it was disbanded.' The Colonel said 'Any man who chose could enlist in any company in the regiment for the war, Captains notwithstanding.' 'Father said I might and mother said I shouldn't,' and I have concluded I would do as I had a mind to.

"Such a feeling pervades the minds of the soldiers [the letter continues] that discipline is played out. Company K refused to turn out to roll call the other morning, and day before yesterday not a man of them appeared on dress parade. Company F would not come out on parade yesterday."

A month later he wrote:

"The Erie Regiment is one grand fizzle out. We left home full of fight, earnestly desiring a chance to mingle with the hosts that fight under the Stars and Stripes. For two months we have drilled steadily, patiently waiting the expected orders which never came but to be countermanded. We have now come to the conclusion that we will have no chance, and are waiting in sullen silence and impatience for the expiration of our time."

It is not surprising that minor disorders should occur. A row broke out in a beer saloon. "Some of the Pittsburgh boys cleaned out the whole thing, broke in the doors, smashed up the glass and furniture." Other troops restored order, inflicting six or eight bayonet wounds. One victim carried a pistol for several days, swearing he would shoot the man who had stabbed him if he could only find out who it was.

The situation is easy to understand. These young men had rushed to save the Union and the Union seemed to scorn them. There was no U. S. O., no visits from Hollywood and Broadway celebrities, no organized sports to keep the men in spirit while Washington unwound red tape and made up its mind.

While Governor Curtin wrangled with the War Department about equipment and quotas, a private in Company C, Tenth Reserve Infantry, did what he could to make his comrades forget their woes. Gib Morgan began telling them tall yarns, as he afterwards put it, "to keep them in heart."

Late in July the Reserves got what they had been clamoring for: a chance to serve in the Army of the United States. When

18

McDowell started toward Bull Run to meet Johnston and Beauregard, Governor Curtin no longer had to urge his troops upon Washington. The Adjutant General notified him that the Reserves were "imperatively needed." The Tenth was mustered into the Federal Army on July 21. They were too late to take part in the Battle of Bull Run, fought on that day, but they got to Washington in time to see some of the wounded brought in. "Many were maimed, and hobbled along as best they could; some were borne upon stretchers, and here and there was one who had lost a leg or an arm." "The sight of these wounded and maimed men," says the historian of Clarion county, "produced a profound impression on the members of the Tenth, and they began to realize the terrible work upon which they were entering."

Before the Tenth was mustered out in June, 1864, they saw as much action as any regiment in the Union armies, and there were many occasions upon which Private Morgan's art was needed to keep them in heart. In October they took their position in the line in Virginia. They fought and suffered casualties at Gaines's Mill, Bull Run, South Mountain, Antietam, Fredericksburg, Gettysburg, Spottsylvania, Bethsada Church. They were twice praised in General Meade's dispatches and once in General Hooker's.

It is impossible to trace in detail Gib Morgan's personal history through the war. In his later years when his little granddaughter would be frightened by a thunderstorm, he would take her on his lap and tell her about the battles he had fought. But to others he was not given to talking about his career as a soldier. He once told John Chambers about an experience under fire, but at that time Gib was already famous as the Munchausen of the Oil Fields, and Chambers catalogued his narrative as another tall tale. He did not know that Gib had been in the army. This may in part explain Gib's reticence.

We may assume that during his three years as a soldier Gib Morgan exhibited the same good nature that characterized his maturity. He liked to play pranks, and he may have been one of the anonymous soldiers who after pay day on June 30, 1862, outwitted a cider vendor who set up for business in a tent near Manassas. This trader retailed his products at ten cents a glass. "Some of the boys considering the price uncommonly large and the glass exceedingly small, determined to set up opposition, and accordingly borrowed an auger and faucet from the sutler, tapped the barrel through the tent at the other end and sold much larger glasses at a much smaller price, and made more money from the operation than the man on the inside."

The author of the *Oil Derrick* obituary says that Gib Morgan was "noted for his bravery." He enlisted as a private and he was honorably discharged as a private. He was on duty as a teamster from June 10, 1863 to April 30, 1864. In July, 1862, near Harrison's Landing, Virginia, he contracted "malarial poisoning" and diarrhoea "from excessive heat, impure water, and improper diet." The official records tell us little more. But if he failed to attain individual mention in the dispatches of the generals, if he failed to receive extraordinary promotion in rank, he became known as "the best story teller in the regiment." Clearly he served his country better than some of the generals who commanded him. He also laid the foundation for his future fame: the Minstrel of the Tenth would in time become the Minstrel of the Oil Industry.

What stories Gib Morgan told his comrades in arms, the records do not reveal, and no survivors of the Tenth remain to tell us. He must, however, have begun with the yarns he had heard around Callensburg and Emlenton as a child: tall tales about hunting and fishing and planting; for although he became America's most fertile inventor of tall tales, to the end of his life he enjoyed telling about such adventures as shooting into a flock of pigeons and being buried in dead birds and fleeing for his life to escape fast-growing cucumber vines.

HOW GIB MORGAN LEARNED THE TRICKS OF THE TRADE AND BECAME A DRILLER

 WHEN GIB MORGAN GOT HOME from the war in June, 1864, the oil excitement was reaching the crest of the first speculative boom. Visitors to the region in 1864 and 1865 write of crowded trains and stage coaches, of hotels, poorer, said a forty-niner who visited the region, than those of the western mining towns, where only a half bed at most could be obtained, of dining rooms where tickets were required for admission. They write of swearing teamsters on traffic-jammed roads where horses sunk to their bellies in mud, of streets that were   Wholly unclassable
Almost impassable
Hardly jackassable.

They write of thousands of derricks spilling over Oil creek valley northeast to Tidioute on the Allegheny, down the Allegheny to Franklin. They write of "sharp-eyed, trim-dressed and eager speculators from New York, Philadelphia, and Pittsburgh, carpet sack in hand, or with travelling bag strapped over the shoulder, going down to secure 'a big thing;' traders anxious to open up a line of custom; rough fellows, going down to work at the wells; and old farmers, coarsely clad . . ., who had within a year or two been made rich by farms that had previously made them poor;" recently discharged soldiers, North and South, looking for work or adventure or both—soldiers in such numbers as to lead David Lowery to remark that though Memorial Day dated only from 1867, the Veterans' Reunion was earlier, the first one, which included men from both sides of the Mason and Dixon Line, being held in Oil Creek valley in 1864.

Gib Morgan was one of the veterans of that reunion. He was now twenty-two years old. He was five feet, nine and half inches tall and weighed a hundred and fifty pounds. With his dark hair and complexion accentuated by lively grey eyes, he was regarded as handsome. Matured by three years of hard military service but recuperated from its rigors, he now faced the future. If he had ever had any desire to escape from his native valley and seek his fortune in the big world, that desire was gone. The world had come to his valley and was surging about him.

"At the close of the hostilities he returned to his native heath to find it in the throes of excitement engendered by the great discovery of Colonel Drake, and he promptly engaged in the oil business and was active in practically every line of its ramifications." Exactly what is to be understood by the phrase "practically every line of its ramifications"—the quotation is from an obituary —is not clear. Certainly Gib Morgan never became a financier or producer on a scale sufficient to attain any prominence. In later years he always referred to himself as a driller and was so put down in the records of the National Archives. And even though there are men who remember him as a tool dresser and who contend that he never got beyond this status, there can be no doubt that he did become a driller; but when he was first employed in this capacity it is impossible to tell. If he began work as a tool dresser or driller's apprentice in 1864, he should have been qualified as a driller before the collapse of the first boom in 1866. He was, however, dressing tools when Jim McCormick, now of Marietta,

21

Ohio, knew him in Bradford in 1878. The truth seems to be that even after he was qualified as a driller Gib would take a subordinate position if no job as driller was available.

Driller or tool dresser, Gib soon learned the tools and techniques that were to figure prominently in the tales that afterwards made him famous.

The rig that he learned to operate, in comparison with the machinery of the present day, was a light and crude affair; yet it was not essentially different from the cable-tool drill in many places still in use. For Drake had not only drilled the first commercial oil well in the United States; he and Uncle Billy Smith, a former salt-well driller, had also shown others how to drill them.

Derricks in the days of Morgan's apprenticeship were usually about forty feet high and ten feet at the base. At the top, on what was called the crown block, were two grooved pulleys, one for the drill cable and one for the sand line. A short distance from the derrick was the power plant, a steam engine of from six to twelve horsepower. A belt led from the engine to a wooden band wheel which turned a crankshaft. Swung to a heavy upright timber, called the Samson post, and pivoting on it, was the walking beam, one end of which was connected to the crank by a pitman. The other end was fastened to the drilling cable, and motion of the beam raised and lowered the tools in the well. Opposite the walking beam, just inside the derrick, was a windlass consisting of a large wooden shaft and two wooden wheels, called the bull shaft and bull wheels respectively, upon which the cable was wound, after the end had been spiked to a yard, or spoke of the bull wheel. The other end of the cable went over the crown pulley and down to the well, where it terminated in a rope bucket, to which the tools were fastened. The connection between the cable and the walking beam was made by the temper screw, one end of which was swung to the beam, and the other clamped to the cable. By turning the temper screw, said to have been an invention of Billy Smith, the driller could lower his tools as the well deepened. When the end of the threads was reached, the clamps were loosened and set higher up on the cable. Thus drillers spoke of drilling a screw, which was about thirty inches.

To protect the driller in case the walking beam should break or become loose, a strong timber was set under the beam just low enough to avoid contact with it. This was called the headache post because, one driller informs me, it prevented headaches when the walking beam broke.

The tools, referred to collectively as a string of tools, consisted of a chisel-like bit, a drill stem, or auger as it was sometimes called although it did not rotate, a pair of jars, a sinker, and a rope socket. The bit was the cutting tool. The purpose of the drill stem was to add weight to give the blow greater force and to add length to make the drilling of a straight hole easier. The jars, also said to have been invented by Uncle Billy Smith, were two long flat links that slid back and forth on each other with a stroke of about fifteen inches. They gave play and caused a light upward stroke and loosened the bit and prevented its sticking in the hole. The sinker resembled a short drill stem. It was placed above the jars.

The early drillers, following Drake's practice, began their wells by driving an iron pipe through the soil to bed rock to prevent caving. Later a large bit was used to penetrate to bed rock, a casing was lowered and set, then drilling continued with the standard bit. Beginning a well came to be known as spudding in. Since the distance from the end of the walking beam to the ground was less than the length of the string of tools, spudding was done with a jerk line. The pitman was disconnected from the crank, to which a cable was attached. The other end of this cable or jerk line was fastened by a slip knot, or a spudding shoe, to the drilling cable, not far above the bull wheels. The turning of the crank thus moved the tools up and down.

Periodically the tools had to be pulled, or withdrawn, for the removal of the detritus, usually called cuttings. During the drilling process, unless a vein had been struck, water was poured or dripped into the whole, diluting the pulverized earth and rock and making a slush. When the tools were withdrawn, the sand bucket (called also the sand pump and the bailer), a tube with a valve in the bottom, was lowered and the slush drawn out.

Sometimes tools were lost in the well by the breaking of a cable or a bit; sometimes they might become stuck in the well. In either event a fishing job was required. A broken cable might be caught with a rope spear let down on the drill stem. A bit might be recovered by a horn socket, a tube with a conical shaped end for slipping it over the bit, and a spring latch for gripping it. If the tools became too fast and could not be loosened by the drilling tools, it might be necessary to put on one or more pairs of long-stroke fishing jars. When this was done the cable was cut near the rope socket by means of special tool let down into the well. Then the horn socket and jars with several sinkers were let down. After

23

the tools were gripped then came the task of jarring them loose.

When the well was completed, casing or tubing must be set. In the early days of the Pennsylvania fields, before the invention of the mechanical packer and before the techniques of cementing were developed, the water above the oil producing stratum was shut off by means of a seed bag. This was a circular leather bag filled with flaxseed. It was fastened about the tubing, and when the seed expanded from moisture, it sealed the space between the tubing and the sides of the well.

During boom times drilling went on twenty-four hours a day, though in the Pennsylvania fields it was customary to shut down on Sunday. Each rig required a crew of four men working by twos in twelve-hour shifts, or tours (pronounced towers), from twelve to twelve. Each shift consisted of a driller, often called the rope choker, and a tool dresser, often called the toolie. The tool dresser was the driller's helper. He kept steam pressure up, he climbed the derrick when the crown pulleys needed oiling, and generally made himself useful around the rig. But his chief duty, the one that gave him his title, was sharpening or dressing the bit. This he did by heating it in a hand forge and pounding it with a sledge hammer. It was important that the bit be properly shaped, otherwise it was liable to stick in the well.

The driller's position was an important one. In the absence of the producer or drilling contractor, he was in full charge of the drilling. Upon his skill depended the successful completion of the well. He must know how to keep the hole straight, often very difficult when hard, inclined strata were encountered, so that it could be cased when completed. He must dig a round hole with a flat bit. As he sat on his high stool under the walking beam with a round stick lashed to the cable, he gave the tools now a quarter turn, now a half turn, first in one direction and then the other. Now and then he would pull his tools and put on a special bit called a reamer, or rimmer, to shape up the sides of the well. At all times the driller must know what was going on down under the ground, and he had nothing to tell him but the feel of the cable to his sensitive hands. He was the most skilled worker in the field, and generally he was intelligent. There are stupid lawyers, stupid business men, stupid doctors, stupid professors; and I suppose there are stupid oil drillers, but they are rare. In an article entitled "The Driller As I Knew Him," one producer, who mentions Gib Morgan as an example, says of the old-time driller: "He is a bright, up-to-date, clever fellow, full of good stories, bubbling over with wit."

The driller knew his own importance and behaved accordingly. If he drank whisky, he drank good whisky. He was fastidious about his dress. He might wear denim on the derrick floor, but even there he was particular about his head and feet. Tool dressers might wear Dayton railroad shoes at a dollar six bits a pair; the driller demanded Wisconsin boots at twelve dollars the pair. He demanded also a good hat, but it must identify him as a driller. This meant that even when he was off duty, his hat must be spattered with slush. "Every other article on his person must be immaculate," wrote a journalist in the Oil City *Derrick*, "but his hat must have the white spots from the sand pump or the wearer did not consider himself dressed up." If necessary he would take a new hat to the slush pit and put on a few spots by hand before he would wear it in public.

He had other extravagances about clothes. In the early days the driller was paid, not every Saturday, but upon completion of the well, when he was handed his money on the derrick floor. On the day when he expected to complete the well and set the tubing, he took his Sunday clothes to the location. As soon as he got his pay, he stripped himself of the clothing he had worn on the job and threw it away. "Boots that cost him twelve dollars per pair were often thrown aside as carelessly as his cheaper overalls." There was generally some bum or other poor person waiting to pick them up. Ninety-one year old Joe Moon, who first knew Gib Morgan in 1887, and who drilled for Dan Moran around Oil City, says, however, that the custom was not so extravagant as it sounds; for when he brought in a good well Moran would make him a present of a new outfit of clothes.

The driller's wit often took the turn of horseplay. One prank often played upon green men was finding some pretext for making them ride the walking beam. Once when Gib was visiting his brother Harrison who was in charge of a lease, a man appeared saying that he had heard that a pumper was needed and that he would like to apply for the job. No, he had had no experience in the oil fields but he was willing to learn. Gib, who really had no authority to hire him, told him that not all men could stand the work of pumping and that the practice was to try them out before hiring them. The applicant was willing. Gib told him that if he could ride the walking beam for an hour he would make a good pumper. As the beam makes about forty strokes to the minute,

25

each terminating in a sharp jar, the candidate came down dizzy and nauseated, saying that he doubted whether he could stand the work.

Gib not only found his vocation. He also fell in love. He married Mary Elizabeth Ritchey in Emlenton on January 20, 1868. Mary, or Mollie as her family called her, was the daughter of James Ritchey of Richland on Ritchey Run, at the mouth of which George Morgan's barge works had been located. Gib in all probability knew her when they were children, and he may have courted her before he went to war. At the time of the marriage, Gib gave his residence as Tionesta, where his father had just moved.

The oil fields were no place to take the bride of a driller, who would be completing a well every month or so and moving to a new location. Housing would be too difficult. There were shack rooming and boarding houses for the men, but some drilling crews preferred to save money by building log huts and batching near the well. Gib left Mollie at Tionesta, and when the Morgan family moved out to Bear Creek, Mollie went with them. The village was less than thirty miles from any point in the field, and Gib could come home between wells, or sometimes when working nearby, on Sunday.

Some of his visits were recorded by the local paper. The Forest county *Republican* on June 14, 1870, notes:

"A few days since we were pleased to meet our old friend Gib Morgan, who formerly lived at Emlenton, but now resides at Bear Creek. Gib was an old army chum, and we trust he will call on us frequently. The latch string is always out for any of our old companions in arms."

The editor does not say so, but the presence of Gib at Bear Creek and Tionesta at that particular time is probably to be accounted for by the birth of a son Charles C., born on June 6. When his eldest, Ed, was born I have not been able to find out. A third son, Warren, was born on February 11, 1872. Mollie never recovered from the birth of Warren. She lingered until April 20 and died.

If Mollie had lived, Gib in all probability would have saved his money, invested it in a small business, and died a respected burgess like his father. Or he might have become the steady employee of

26

some stable producer and in time retired on a pension and spent his last years in a pleasant cottage in Emlenton, Pennsylvania, Jamestown, New York, or Marietta, Ohio, as a good many of his contemporaries did. But, as he used to tell his granddaughter, it seemed like his luck changed when Mollie died. He never could settle down again. He became a rover, a gipsy driller, as one man called him, and spent the next twenty years roaming from field to field, and back again, never staying very long anywhere. And wherever he went he carried his stories with him.

HOW GIB MORGAN BECAME THE WANDERING MINSTREL OF THE OIL FIELDS

 OF COURSE GIB COULD NOT CONSIDER taking his children with him to the oil fields. He left them with the Ritchey family until Warren was about four years old. Then they went to live with George Cubbison and his wife, who was a sister of James Ritchey. Here they remained until they were grown, attending in due time the public schools of Tionesta, Scrubgrass, and McCoy near Emlenton.

As the boys grew up, they went their various ways and Gib gradually lost contact with Ed and Charley. While he was still a youngster, Ed went to the Pacific coast. His letters home became more and more infrequent, and eventually stopped. Gib must have eventually received word of his death, for when in 1887 he listed his living children, he put down only Charles and Warren. Charley married in Pennsylvania and had a son, whom he named Ed. When Ed was about six years old, his father mysteriously disappeared, and Gib never heard from him again. Warren was enough like his father to receive the nickname of Little Gib. After he was grown the Little was often dropped and he was called Gib, a fact which has occasioned the writer of this sketch considerable trouble. Warren married Elizabeth Gordon and established his home at Eau Claire. Like his father, he became an oil well driller and later a drilling contractor. He followed oil development into the Southwest and died in Wichita Falls, Texas, in 1912. He left a daughter, Edna, who now lives at Butler, Pennsylvania.

To detail Gib Morgan's wanderings in the oil fields of various states from 1872 to 1892 would not serve the purpose of this sketch even if the information were available. During all this time he regarded Emlenton as his "home and headquarters." For a while he stayed near his children. He was in Edinburgh, now Knox, in his native county during a part of the seventies. He was remembered there, among others, by John H. Altman, then a pumper, but later a drilling contractor, who used to tell his children —he had nine—Gib Morgan stories at bed time. "These stories," writes Mrs. B. H. McMullen, of Oil City, "have many times been the means of getting four or five of us asleep at night." Gib must have considered Edinburgh more or less his home, for one West Virginian refers to him as "that old liar of Gib Morgan from Edinburgh, Clarion Co., Penna." Old timers remember that once in a hotel bar near Edinburgh, a local farmer, entranced by Gib's yarns, interrupted to ask, "Stranger, who might you be?" "Amanca," replied Gib. "Sall Amanca is my half-sister."

Since Salamanca, New York, was not far away, the joke was not lost.

When the "Mystery" well on tract 646 came in near Cherry Grove at the rate of 3600 barrels a day in 1882, Gib was among the hundreds that rushed to the field. C. R. Boyd, who was born nearby in Tiona more than seventy years ago, remembers him there as working for a pipe line company, clearing and grading a plot of ground on Tionesta creek for storage tanks. When Bradford began booming in 1876, Gib went there. Jim McCormick knew him in that field as a tool dresser in 1878. But G. L. Kerr of Bradford insists that he was a driller "and a good one."

Kerr says that once when Gib was pulling the tools preparatory to bailing out, he told the tool dresser to "stab the bailer" into the well.

"You can't do that," said the tool dresser. "How will it pass the tools?"

"That's the bailer's business," replied Gib.

When Macksburg, Ohio, boomed in 1882 and 1883, Gib was there. He is yet well remembered in the village, and the tendency of the people to make him a hero is evidenced by the persistence of a tradition that he was a driller on the Rice No. 1, the first deep producer in the field. His yarns and wisecracks are still repeated when old timers gather at Longfellow's general store.

When Gib was around Macksburg, an agent came into the boom town selling Texas "farm" lands. Gib was convinced that the man was a swindler. So on one occasion when the dealer in land had a group about him and was painting in glorious colors the fertility of the quarter sections he had for sale, Gib spoke up to tell about his visit to Texas. His host, Gib said, was showing him his farm. As they were walking across a corn field, it suddenly got dark, although it was mid-afternoon. Cows came lowing home to be milked and chickens went to roost.

"Don't worry," said the Texan; "it will be light again in a few minutes."

By this time Gib had discovered that the clouds which had given the day the darkness of night were swarms of grasshoppers. They lit on the corn field, tarried a few minutes and were gone. So was the corn. Every blade had been eaten, and even the stalks into the ground.

Now except for the locale this was no tall tale. Gib had never been to Texas, and Texas had never experienced any such grass-hopper plague as he described. But the Oil City *Derrick* on March 5, 1877, had carried a notice of the arrival of destitute families who had been, as the *Derrick* put it, "grasshopped out" on the great plains. Their men sought work in the oil fields, and Gib had probably heard them describe the swarms of locusts that grass-hopped them out.

But the men around Macksburg thought Gib's tale a good one, and after that when the land agent would approach a customer, there would be winking and laughter and slapping of knees. So far as my informants know, no sales were made.

Gib seems to have adopted Texas while he was at Macksburg. Once when health was the topic of conversation, Gib told the crowd around the boarding house how his sister-in-law down in Texas kept physically fit: she walked a barbed wire fence every morning barefooted with a wildcat under each arm.

Gib, like his father, must have kept himself posted on what was going on. Wire fence began to be used on a large scale in Texas in 1881.

But the joke that he is best remembered for in Macksburg is one that shows that he was already noted for his tall lies. As he was passing one day on his way to tour, someone stopped him and said, "Gib, tell us a lie."

With a show of deep emotion, Gib said, "I can't tell you a lie now. I've just got word that the cable clamps have slipped and killed my brother at the well."

Deeply humbled the man expressed his regrets and Gib went on.

29

Not many minutes behind him came a crowd seeking more information about the accident. They found Gib calmly at work.

"You told us your brother had been killed," they accused.

"You asked for a lie, didn't you?" Gib replied.

This is the story as I heard it in Macksburg. As a matter of fact, Gib had no brother in the field. What he probably said was "buddy," meaning the driller on the other tour.

When Gib left the Marietta field I do not know. In 1886 his brother Harrison was living at Alum Rock, near Emlenton. Mrs. J. M. Taylor, Harrison's step-daughter, remembers that Gib used to visit them sometimes between wells, and that once he stayed for a considerable period while recovering from a burn received in an oil well fire. She does not know in what field Gib was working when he was burned.

He was probably in Oil City. At any rate he was there during the stormy year of 1887 when the bottom dropped out of the crude oil market, and the struggle between the producers and Standard Oil, by then their only purchaser of any consequence, reached a crisis. Finally a truce was reached whereby Standard agreed to sell its surplus of five million barrels to the producers at forty-two cents a barrel, this oil to be held off the market until the price should rise, the producers to get the benefit of the raise. On its part the Producers' Association was to restrict production by a specified amount. To this end all wells were shut down and drilling stopped on November 1.

Gib was employed by a producer who either was not a member of the Association or meant to violate the agreement. The rig was set up and Gib was to spud in the next morning. But when he reached the location the next day, all he found where the derrick had been was a huge crater. If the agreement couldn't stop operations, a heavy charge of nitroglycerin would.

Some time before 1890 Gib was back in Clarion county drilling at Hardy. Then when oil development came to Indiana and northwest Ohio, Gib was there. He worked for Charles A. Reeser, who became his lifelong friend, sometime before November, 1891. Not many months before or after this date he was working for J. S. Boggs at North Baltimore, Ohio.

He spent September, October, and November of 1890 at McDonald, about twenty miles southwest of Pittsburgh, where a new field had been brought in. Harry W. Graham, another driller, and Gib arrived there together. They found all the hotels and rooming houses full, but rented sleeping space in the hay mow of a farmer's barn. This was no hardship to Gib. By this time he had become a boomer, that is a worker who followed flush production, who enjoyed the excitement of new fields, who preferred the crowding and the mud of a new oil town to the more comfortable but staid monotony of a mature field.

In the spring of 1892 he was in Allegheny, but he was back at McDonald in September. He was present there when on the thirteenth Greenlee and Frost's No. 2 Noble Heirs came in at a hundred and fifty barrels an hour. He was a spectator, however, and not a member of the crew that drilled the well. Writes J. P. DeWalt:

> I saw Gib in McDonald, Pa., in September, 1892. I remember very well. Barney Frost and C. D. Greenlee drilled a very large well, estimated at 15,000 barrels daily. They shut the gates on account of no tankage and the gas pressure blew up the connections, and the oil was throwing a solid stream about 150 [feet] in the air. The crew and extra help was trying to shut it in. Mr. Greenlee came up through the woods toward the well with an umbrella to keep the spray off of him. Gib was sitting on a stump watching the workers. He had on a hickory shirt and jeans pants. Mr. Greenlee says, "Gid, why don't you go to work and help close the well. We are paying $1,000 an hour." Gib raised up and said, "Mr. Greenlee, do you suppose I could spoil these clothes for $1,000 per hour?"
>
> I was drilling on the adjoining location at the time.

But most of the two-year period from 1890 to 1892 Gib seems to have spent in West Virginia. He came to Manhattan soon after the excitement following the completion of the first successful wildcat there in 1889. But he also drilled a well or two at Duke Center near Bradford. Some of my informants think that this was the last drilling he did before his retirement.

By the end of 1892 he seems to have been pretty much down and out as a driller. He opened some sort of small business in Sistersville, West Virginia, where he lived in "a little shack along the river." Grant Emory, who was drilling nearby, remembers it as a small confectionery. J. M. Curry, who was also there, refers to it as a "lemonade stand." His place was a favorite hangout for

31

the younger oil field workers, who gathered there to hear Gib's stories, but he does not seem to have prospered. He had filed a declaration for a Civil War pension in September, 1887, but had abandoned the claim. He filed a second declaration on April 20, 1890, under the new act passed that year. His claim was not adjudicated and his certificate issued until November 15, 1897, when he was awarded six dollars a month retroactive to April 20, 1890.

Under the act it was not necessary for a veteran to take a pauper's oath. He must show only that he was "suffering from some mental or physical disability—not the result of vicious habits —rendering him unable to earn a living by manual labor." Having an income from sources other than from manual labor in no way debarred one from drawing a pension.

In his original declaration Gib had stated that while near "Harrison's Landing" in Virginia, he ". . . contracted chronic malarial poisoning resulting [in] chronic diarrhœa under the following circumstances: from excessive heat impure water & improper diet." Pension rates ranged from six to twelve dollars a month, depending on the degree of disability. Gib's six-dollar allowance indicated that his disability was accounted fifty per cent.

During 1893 and a part of 1894 Gib lived with his son Warren at Eau Claire, Pennsylvania. In 1894 he was admitted to the National Home for Disabled Soldiers at Marion, Indiana. His days of roaming were by no means over, but from this time until his death, his home was to be one or another of the soldiers' homes.

If Gib was exceptional in retiring from active drilling at the age of fifty, he was exceptional in the length of his career rather than in the brevity of it. Then as now the oil worker's game was a young man's game. Few men spend twenty-eight years on the walking beam.

What part liquor played in Gib's wandering career and in his retirement is not clear. Theoretically he could not have got a pension if his disability had been due to excessive use of alcohol. And if he was ever discharged for drunkenness, it has slipped the memory of the men who knew him.

They do remember him, however, as a man who liked his liquor, and as one who would have been better off if he had consumed less.

"Did he drink?" I asked G. L. Kerr of Bradford.

"Yes, moderately," was the reply.

"Yes, he did like his liquor," is the testimony of another witness.

32

C. R. Boyd, who knew him in Cherry Grove in 1882, describes him as "a convivial soul," adding that in modern parlance "he would probably be classed as a bum or bar-fly." W. G. Long, the producer whose article on "The Driller As I Knew Him" has already been cited, has high praise for Gib Morgan's wit and invention. He says, "But for the intemperate use of John Barley-corn, he might have stood today beside Artemus Ward, Bill Nye, or Samuel L. Clemens; instead he spent his declining years in the Soldiers' Home. . . ." And in Warren Morgan's family it was said that liquor prevented Gib from realizing his full potentialities.

Certainly the conditions under which the early drilling crews worked were not conducive to teetotalism. The long twelve-hour day and the custom of paying off when the well was completed meant that after from one to three months of hard labor, the driller found himself temporarily at leisure with a considerable sum of money in his pocket. Like the cowboy after a long drive from Texas to Dodge City, he was likely to go on a spree, big or little, before he settled down to work again. Some spent all their money, some only a part.

Some became so addicted that they could not wait for the completion of the well. One of these, a man named Jack Bradley, attained considerable fame under the nom de guerre of Big Hole Jack. Big Hole Jack insisted that it was beneath his dignity to work on any well smaller than ten inches in diameter. He would spud in and set the first casing, but when it came time to put on a bit smaller than ten inches, he would draw his time and go to town. Now any cable tool driller will tell you that the first hundred feet are normally the hardest. With plenty of cable in the ground the driller can tell by the feel of it how his hole is doing. But it was not, according to old timers, pride in the size of the hole or in doing a difficult job, as he pretended that made Big Hole Jack ask for his time. It was that he always got dry and drew his pay to go on a spree.

To those who had money, facilities for a spree were always available. In each new field saloons multiplied as derricks did. In the early sixties, however, the citizens of the oil regions managed to keep the sale of liquor at a minimum. There was relatively little lawlessness in the oil fields before 1865. Then, the war over, there came an influx of all kinds of dissolute characters such as followed later oil booms and gave oil towns an exaggerated reputation for wickedness. In established communities like Titusville, they were

33

kept in check by vigilant citizens, whose armed committees not
infrequently ordered undesirables to leave town permanently. In
fields where there was no municipal government they were less
successfully dealt with, and in some short-lived communities like
Pit Hole lawlessness subsided only when oil ceased flowing and
the population left.

Gib Morgan, however, had no truck with lawlessness. He was
never a patron of cheap concert saloons, gambling dens, bawdy
houses or other low dives. There survives no memory or tradition
of disorderly conduct on his part. What coarseness there is in the
tales arises from references to bodily processes and the use of
barnyard language. Not one of them involved sex. The unanimous
testimony is that he was always in a good humor. "He was never
quarrelsome when drinking," says Grant Emory, who knew him
in West Virginia, "just liked to tell big stories." "Perfectly harm-
less either sober or drinking—never knew him to have a fight,"
says another driller who knew him. I have asked several what Gib
did if a victim of one of his jokes got angry and wanted to fight.
"Tell him a tall tale and make him laugh," said one. 'But it wasn't
often that Gib made anybody angry, and when he did, he could
count on the sympathy of the crowd.

Gib's dissipation consisted merely in sitting around hotel bars
and saloons, talking to his friends, telling stories to those who
cared to listen, treating and being treated, when by the canons of
capitalistic society he should have been working harder and saving
his money. He seems, especially after his fame as a raconteur had
spread through the oil regions, to have been the treatee more
often than the treator. Harry Botsford, in an article in the
Saturday Evening Post for October 3, 1942, constructs a scene
such as might have been witnessed at Pleasantville, Pennsylvania,
in the 1890's. Morgan is represented as standing at the hotel bar
with a tumbler and a partially empty bottle. Amid the general
conversation he drinks in silence until another bottle is set before
him. Gradually he is induced to unlock his word hoard and launch
into a series of tales. The testimony of dozens of other men
confirm the typicality of this scene.

Gib was generally well liked and both workers and producers
were willing to buy him liquor to keep talking. "He would hang
around saloons," writes C. H. Halderman, "and if they would buy
or give him a few drinks, he could start and reel off some comic
stories or tales. He could make them up in his mind and tell them
so they were comic."

34

Many of Gib's wisecracks had to do with his taste for liquor and the meagerness of his worldly goods.

Once as he and his tool dresser were going on tour at noon, they met a boiler truck on its way to a new location. Gib stopped, walked around the heavy wagon, looking at it from every angle as though to make sure that no detail of its construction escaped him.

"Come on," said the tool dresser. "We'll be late on tour."

Gib continued to scrutinize the wagon. "What on earth are you looking at that boiler wagon for?" asked the tool dresser.

"I was just thinking of buying one like it to move my trunk from one boarding house to another."

Gib used to create a good deal of laughter by telling how he came to quit drinking. Once he said an angel appeared to him in a vision and converted him to the cause of temperance. Another time he said he quit because he woke up in the night and found the walls of his room covered with cross-eyed bugs. Once he said he quit because of something he saw in his glass. Just as he was about to drink he looked down and noticed a little pink pig swimming around in his liquor. As Gib would be standing at the bar with a bottle and glass before him when he said these things, they were regarded as very, very funny.

He did abstain for a considerable period of time while he was running his confectionery at Sistersville. As J. M. Curry remembers it, Gib was completely off liquor. He had taken in an old friend as partner, and when this friend got drunk, Gib dissolved or threatened to dissolve the partnership.

As would be expected, the attitudes of Gib's surviving acquaintances toward him depend upon their respective scales of values. One driller who had hoarded his money, invested it wisely or luckily, and had retired when his estate reached a hundred thousand dollars, was somewhat contemptuous of Gib. On the other hand, some operators considerably more wealthy professed an admiration for him. He was generally liked and admired by the rank and file. "He sure was smart; he sure was smart," one eighty-year old driller kept repeating. Back in the eighties one youngster who came to work in the oil fields took advantage of Gib's popularity to save himself the hazing green hands were subject to. He said that his name was Morgan and that he was Gib Morgan's son come to learn his father's trade. He was immediately accepted as one of the group. Then after a few days he confessed that his name was Reid Imbrie and that he knew Gib Morgan only by reputation. But by this time the men around the boarding houses had learned to like him, and he was spared the usual initiation ceremonies.

Besides being liked for his good nature and for his stories, Gib was respected for his integrity. In gathering these tales I have been reminded many times that Gib never lied to deceive. His old friend Dr. W. M. Kennedy of Franklin wrote:

> They used to say that he was 'the biggest liar in the oil country.' I don't think this is the proper title for him. I would say that the 'best entertainer in the oil country' would have been a much better title.

This judgment is in keeping with contemporary newspaper estimates of his character.

> He was [says the Titusville Herald] an honest man at heart, and when in matters of business or importance he spoke, is was always to tell the truth. But gather about him a group of teentative [sic] listeners and he would put the writer of Arabian Nights to blush.
>
> Although noted for 'stretching the long bow' [says the Oil City Derrick] on occasions when he knew he would not be taken seriously, his word in business matters or between friends was held inviolate.

Gib was a man of integrity and imagination. If he had lived in the days of Charlemagne, he would have been an honored troubadour. The Gilded Age tolerated his art, but offered him no security. This boon eventually came from the Federal Government, not because the Government wished to patronize art, but because the Artist happened to have fought in the Civil War.

HOW GIB MORGAN SPENT HIS DECLINING YEARS AND HOW HIS FAME INCREASED

WHEN GIB WAS ADMITTED TO THE National Home for Disabled Soldiers in 1894, he had the assurance of a roof over his head, clothes that he was proud to wear, and medical care; and if the food was not always to his liking it was at least plentiful and wholesome. His pension was increased from time to time. On June 30, 1900, it

was raised to eight dollars a month, retroactive to April 29, 1899. Again on February 25, 1905, it was raised to ten dollars, retroactive to October 19, 1904. Finally in May, 1907, it was raised to the maximum of twelve dollars a month. The pension never made him rich, but it was pocket money, more than he could spend around the Home. And he had the association of fellow veterans who liked his stories, though they must have heard them many times. When D. M. Hosack was living near Marion, Indiana, in 1901, he used to go to the Home to see Gib. What he remembers most vividly is a thin, wiry man weighing about a hundred and twenty-five pounds seated on the lawn surrounded by some two hundred other veterans listening to his yarns. Gib had been at the Home for more than six years then, but he still had an audience.

On the whole, life was good at the Home. It's chief drawback was monotony. For Gib at heart was still the rambler, the gipsy driller, and the wandering minstrel of the oil fields. He asked for and obtained a transfer to another branch of the Home. Late in August, 1901, he was assigned to Danville, Illinois; then, in 1904, he went to Mountain Home, Johnson City, Tennessee. This he was content to call home the rest of his life. The Home is situated near the North Carolina border in the Appalachian Mountains. It is surrounded by scenery that reminded him of the hills and valleys of Clarion and Venango counties, where he used to hunt as a boy and where he first learned to knock out a temper screw. Behind the Home rose Buffalo and Cherokee Heights; within sight was Roan Mountain, six thousand feet above the sea: It was easy for Gib to feel at home here.

But Gib was not willing to spend all the days of his life anywhere, not even in Johnson City. At least once, in 1906, he went back to Danville to visit his former comrades there. J. P. DeWalt and a friend were strolling through the grounds when they saw a group of old soldiers sitting on benches. "We walked over," he writes, "and there was Gib Morgan spinning a yarn."

Each summer he would get a furlough and journey back to the oil country of Pennsylvania. His annual homecoming became a sort of institution, a triumphal entry. His first stop would be Pittsburgh. There he would register at the Bowyer Hotel, long the favorite hostelry of the oil fraternity. The *Pittsburgh Gazette*, which had featured oil news from the beginning, would learn of his presence (no doubt with Gib's cooperation) and would publish a story in which Gib would be linked with the first robin of spring. Gib's old friends would begin dropping in.

"Where you putting up, Gib?" some veteran driller would ask.

"Under the Sixth Street Bridge," Gib would reply.

Same old Gib. Always wisecracking, always pulling jokes.

Other oil men would drop in—young drillers and tool dressers and producers—who had heard of Gib and were eager for a look, impatient to hear his tales. But Gib wouldn't be rushed. Everything in due time. Somebody would propose a drink. They would file into the bar room. Bottles and glasses would be set out. After a few minutes of decorous reticence, Gib would launch out on his marvelous adventures in Pennsylvania, West Virginia, and other places he had been; in Texas, Baku, the Fiji Islands, and other places he had never been.

After a few days in Pittsburgh Gib would take the train for the oil country—Emlenton, Franklin, Oil City—repeating his triumphal entry into Pittsburgh, coming back to old friends who had known him since he was knee high to a duck. He had a reputation to keep up. Once in Emlenton he was sitting with some friends on the curb in front of a store. Above the store were some offices, one of which was occupied by the dentist and another of which was being remodeled for a new tenant. Carpenters were hammering and sawing. A woman, a newcomer in Emlenton who did not know Gib, approached. She had a rag tied around her swollen jaw. When Gib saw her coming, he assumed an attitude of great pain.

"Can you tell me where the dentist's office is?" asked the woman.

"His office is up there," said Gib. "I went up to see him myself, but when I saw what he was doing to the man in the chair I came down again."

Pleasant as it was around Emlenton and Oil City, Gib would not be too long in getting up to Eau Claire in Butler county. That was where Warren lived. But in all probability Warren would not be at home. He had taken to the temper screw himself and had done well, soon passing from driller to drilling contractor. He spent most of his time now down in Oklahoma and Texas. But Elizabeth would be at Eau Claire, and she liked Gib and always made him feel welcome. Many a time she had suggested that he leave the Home and live with them in Eau Claire. Gib wouldn't hear to that, but it was a fine place to come back to. Elizabeth

knew how to feed a man. What he needed was fried stuff—
buckwheat cakes, ham and eggs, steak and French fried potatoes
—not the gruels and stews they fed him at the Home. That was
invalid's food.

And there was Edna, the only grandchild he knew. Strange the
way he felt about her. It might have been because she thought he
was a great and good man and trusted in him and believed what-
ever he told her. For some reason he would never tell her his tall
tales from the oil fields—only true stories, mostly about the war.
He knew, though, that she knew he was called a great liar. When
Edna got to stretching blanket a little too for, when she said that
there were a million cats in the alley when there were only three,
her mother would say, "Now, Gib! Now, Gib!" But Gib didn't
mind and Edna didn't mind. They were friends and when he told
her how the Tenth was caught in the Rebel fire at Bethshada
Church, she knew he was telling the truth. In his war narratives
he was modest, almost shy, and never made himself the hero.

He loved Edna's dog, a jet-black, curly-haired spaniel named
Fido, who never forgot him from one summer to the next. When
Gib would come home, Fido would run to meet him, barking and
wagging his tail and jumping all over him; while he was there
Fido would follow him everywhere he went, and he would have
gone away with him if he could. The last time Gib left, it looked
as though Fido knew it was the last. They had to put him in the
house to keep him from following Gib to the railway station.
Elizabeth and Edna were sitting at the window waving goodbye.
There was frost in the air, and window panes were covered with
vapor. Fido ran around the room barking and whining. Then he
crawled up between Edna and her mother and licked the vapor
from the window and watched Gib out of sight. Gib saw him. He
wrote back from Mountain Home: "Good old Fido. Give him
a pet for me."

Gib never came without gifts. He always had a pocket full of
chewing gum, something that Edna's mother would not ordinarily
let her have when she was a wee girl because she swallowed it.
Discipline relaxed a little when Gib came. There would be more
substantial gifts too—toys, fancy hair ribbons, kid gloves, which
her mother thought she was too young to have. Gib's pension
wasn't much, but he always had enough for presents. Once when
he received a considerable sum in arrears, he really spread himself.
For Elizabeth he bought a new Brussels carpet with roses on it for

the parlor, and for Edna, then only five years old, a watch, a real Elgin watch with gold case and jewels on the inside.

Gib never forgot Dave Mitchell's family either, out on the farm near Emlenton. Gib and Dave were great cronies. They had grown up together there around Emlenton, and they both had been through the Civil War. Dave had served in the Sixty-third, but they had seen a great deal of each other and had fought together at Charles City, Malvern Hill, Harrison's Landing and Gettysburg. Dave's son, Charley was now married and had a family. His youngest child, Clara, was about Edna's age. Gib would spend a few days with Charley, and they would drive in town every morning in the buggy, taking Clara with them. Gib was always teasing Clara. When they crossed the Allegheny bridge, he would tell her that he was going to throw Charley out of the buggy. She would beg him not to, and as they neared the end of the long high bridge, Gib would relent and agree to spare Charley this time. Of course Clara knew that he was really joking, but she would feel relieved when Gib would say, "Well, since you don't want me to, I guess I won't throw him out this time." When they got to town Gib would buy her nice presents, generally something to wear. She never will forget the time he came during her fifth year. He took her into a store and had her fitted out—a red dress, a pair of kid gloves, and a pair of Buster Brown shoes with a pencil box thrown in. She knew Gib really wasn't any kin to her, but it seemed like he ought to be her uncle or something. . . .

Gib still had the soldier's and the driller's pride in his personal appearance. His hair was getting thin on top and he did not like it. Although he had satirized patent medicines in some of his best-known tales, he was a sucker for hair restorers. He bought every new tonic that a barber recommended. He wore the blue uniform of a Civil War veteran, and always kept it pressed and the brass buttons shining like new-minted gold pieces. Once when he expected to be in Eau Claire for not more than a day or two, he brought only one uniform and it got so wrinkled that he was ashamed to wear it to town. Edna offered to press it, and Gib went to bed while she worked on the pants. Now Edna didn't know much about pressing pants and she put the creases on the sides instead of the front and back of the legs. When she brought them to Gib, he looked puzzled for a moment and thanked her most graciously. He was about to put them on when Elizabeth came into the room and saw them and began laughing. Gib would have worn them before he would have hurt Edna's feelings.

Gib still drank some too, though never at Elizabeth's house. Not that she was rabid on the subject of liquor. Once when he was there he wanted to go to the Butler County fair at Franklin with Dave Mitchell. At first Elizabeth wouldn't give her consent. She was afraid the excitement would be too much for his heart, especially since a lot of his old friends, including members of the G. A. R. would be wanting to buy him drinks. But Gib swore he would be temperate and she gave in. When he failed to return that night she was a little worried, but not much, for she thought he had probably decided to spend the night at Charley Mitchell's. The next morning she was surprised to see him coming from town. He said they had brought him back the night before, but as he came up the walk he noticed that he was a little unsteady on his feet, so he had gone to the hotel and taken a room. He couldn't embarrass a lady.

Sometimes Gib had difficulty in making his money last until his furlough was over. But when his money was all spent he still got along very well. It was undestood that when he drank with the oil field crowd, the drinks were always on somebody else. They might be on the house, they might be on some producer he had worked for, they might be on young drillers and roughnecks and pipe line gang men who had heard his tales from the veterans and now came to hear the master himself. But they were never on Gib. If any of these newcomers forgot or were ignorant of the customs of the service, Gib had a way of reminding them. He told them about his battle with the Whickles.

The whickles were strange insects, the description of which might vary from time to time. As Harry Botsford heard Gib's narrative, they were a cross between a canary and a bumblebee, and Gib felt a keen responsibility for their existence, since it was his own escaped female canary that mated with a bumblebee and founded the species. The staple diet of the whickles was crude petroleum. Gib had seen them flying down into a well in a steady stream on one side and out in a steady stream on the other. That was why the wells in the Pennsylvania field were failing. If there was anything whickles liked better than crude oil it was apple-jack, and Gib was using their addiction to this drink as a means of saving the oil industry. He would sprinkle apple-jack on the bushes around the oil wells; the whickles would come and get drunk, and Gib would catch them. As Botsford tells the story, Gib had gone to Harrisburg and seen the governor and got him to put a bounty on whickle scalps. But as they told me the story in Emlenton and Marietta, Gib, out of the mere generosity of his heart and his interest to the public welfare, was making a heroic effort to save the oil industry of his native state. Of course apple-jack was expensive, and Gib's means were limited. . . . The hint was sufficient.

If need be, Gib could obtain board and lodging in the same way he obtained drinks. In the fall of 1897 John C. Chambers then a youngster with ninety dollars cash, ninety days' credit and a lot of enthusiasm, opened a general store in the new oil field at Klondike, McKean county, Pennsylvania. Gib Morgan turned up in the field and got to coming into Chamber's store. And when Gib came to the store, customers came. Gib did not go back Home that winter. Chambers paid for his room and board until June just to have him around as an added attraction to his customers.

It would be misleading, however, to imply that Gib always held his audience spellbound—eager, breathless, oblivious to all save the words of the minstrel. But when his audience did desert him, he was not consumed by self-pity.

Since the tool dresser was an apprentice to the driller, he was given an opportunity to handle the cable from time to time. After he had learned the rudiments of "rope choking," the driller would often leave him in charge if he wished to be away from the well for a half hour or so. The speech formula was "You watch her a while," or "You watch her while I go do so and so." If the tool dresser wished to volunteer, he would say, "You go ahead, I'll watch her."

Now this is the reason for putting in this information here: once when Gib was a guest at an oil workers' boarding house (whether paying or non-paying my informant does not know), he was in the midst of a yarn when the dinner bell rang. The men rushed into the dining room without so much as waiting for Gib to finish the sentence he was speaking—all except one, a youth who followed the crowd reluctantly, looking back at Gib apologetically.

"Go ahead," said Gib. "I'll watch her."

For several years after his retirement, Gib could still choke a cable and do his twelve-hour tour along with a younger man, at least for a month or two. If urged sufficiently he might take a job. In 1896 a sixteen-year-old boy named Frank James got a job hauling wood to fire the boilers on the Duckworth lease near Montpelier, Indiana. Gib had got a furlough from the Home at Marion and was drilling on the same lease. James, now a retired driller of Peru, Kansas, is still proud of having been initiated into the oil game on a lease where Gib Morgan was working. When approached by a producer or drilling contractor, Gib would simulate complete indifference. Once when there was a shortage of drillers in the Indiana field, a contractor went to Gib and said, "Gib, why don't you help me out? You're a driller, arent you?"

"Am I a driller?" exclaimed Gib. "Why, man, I drilled on one well eight years."

Gib traveled about more than usual in 1908. He made his customary trip to the oil region of Pennsylvania. There he met a friend, a driller by the name of Hood, who was getting ready to go to Bartlesville, Oklahoma, to look for work. He suggested that Gib come along and look for a job too. Gib went, not for the job but for the trip. He enjoyed the train ride and got to see a part of Oklahoma, and he had had a pleasant visit with Warren. This was probably as far into the Southwest as Gib ever got; for although some of his tales have a Texas setting, there is no evidence that he was ever in the state.

But Gib's wandering was about over. He had suffered a sun stroke in 1901, and his health had been gradually declining since. Reports of examining physicians on file in the National Archives reveal an increasing complication of ailments. In the summer of 1908 he was too weak to make his usual trip back to his old haunts. The end came on February 19, 1909, the certificate attributing his death immediately to "mitral insufficiency," which in lay language means leakage of the heart. Pursuant to his own request, he was given military burial at the Mountain Home Cemetery.

THE MYSTERY OF GIB MORGAN'S BOOK

GIB MORGAN MUST HAVE BEEN told hundreds of times that he ought to put his stories in a book. The idea appealed to him and he toyed with it for fifteen years or more, and there is a persistent legend that he actually wrote the book.

Edna Morgan believes that her father used to have in his possession a book written by Gib Morgan. He carried it with him to the Southwest, but when his personal belongings were sent from Wichita Falls after his death in 1912, the book was not among them. Another witness is John C. Chambers of Chanute, Kansas, who was Gib's patron in 1897-98. Writing on March 20, 1942, Mr. Chambers says: "Years ago I purchased a book of stories by Gib Morgan. I may have it but [I am] not sure, as it was over twenty years ago, while I was living in Indianapolis." I interviewed Mr. Chambers a month later. He had not been able to find the book, but he thought it was published in 1916, possibly by the *Derrick* in Oil City. Chambers fixed the date of publication by the date of his residence in Indianapolis. If he is right, the book he recalls could be the one Edna Morgan has in mind only if it were a reprint or a later edition.

A third witness is Louis Wolford of Macksburg, Ohio, who knew Gib there in 1883-84. Mr. Wolford says that he once read a book by Gib Morgan. He does not remember the title or the date of publication. He says he bought it from a news butcher on the train and it lay around the house for years, but he doesn't know what became of it.

These are the persons who believe that they have seen Gib Morgan's published book. There is another school of thought, the school of the lost manuscript.

Ed Nason of Warren, Pennsylvania, son of Charles Nason, a driller of Gib Morgan's generation and reputed author of a famous oil field poem entitled "the Driller's Dream," remembers once having seen "a pamphlet which was a compendium of Morgan stories." He says also that "Gib Morgan started to write a book of his adventures many times, but each time, after becoming drunk, he destroyed the manuscript." But as D. M. Hosack had the story from Warren Morgan after Gib's death (that is between 1909 and 1912), Gib was writing a book to be entitled *Ten Years Under the Beam,* and "had it about finished when some one got him drunk and got away with the book and it was never heard from."

Dozens of my informants thought they remembered seeing some of Gib's yarns in print not only in the oil field press, where they appeared as feature stories on the occasions of his summer visits, but also in the catalogue of some oil field supply company. While a search through such catalogues was under way, I was advised by J. M. Gordon of Emlenton to look for a book published by S. W. Munn of Mannington, West Virginia. This proved to be the book so many had remembered.

S. W. Munn had been associated with Gib in the oil fields. He had gone to the Oil Creek country in 1867 and had got a job boating oil down the river. He later became a driller and worked in the various fields in which Gib was working. In 1892 he bought an interest in the Union Drilling Company at Washington, Pennsylvania. In 1896 he moved to Mannington, where he specialized in fishing. He patented two inventions, a joint indicator and a casing cutter. To advertise his fishing business he issued in 1898 and again in 1900 an almanac-like booklet of one hundred and ninety pages, entitled *Useful Information for Oil Men.* The 1900 edition contains "A Letter From My Old Friend Gib Morgan" and "Some Stories by Gib Morgan," occupying pages 23 to 28.

Gib's stories might have been printed in the advertising of other firms, but if so I have been unable to find them. Nor have I been able to find the book Edna Morgan remembers as a child, nor the book that John Chambers read in 1916, nor the book that Louis Wolford bought on the train. The fact that I am unable to find a book is no proof that it does not exist; yet I am inclined to believe that Gib's book was never published. I think it is possible that the book Edna Morgan remembers is Munn's *Useful Information for Oil Men* or a bound manuscript. Chambers and Wolford might have had *Useful Information* in mind..

There is, however, another possibility. A novel by Charles Oliver, entitled *646 and the Troubleman,* published by Rand McNally in 1916, has in it a character called "Fighting Gib," who has no fights in the story and who, though he is not allowed to tell a single tall tale, seems nevertheless to have been suggested by Gib Morgan. This book could easily have been associated in Chambers' mind with Gib Morgan and hence with his tales.

If Gib's book was published it somehow escaped the notice of the oil region press. The Oil City *Derrick* obituary says that "upon the occasion of his last visit to Oil City, nearly two years since, 'Gib' confessed that he has been devoting his spare time to their [the tales'] compilation with the object of publishing them in book form." In 1907, then, Gib was working on his manuscript. If it had been published before his death in 1909, that fact should have been known to the proprietor of the *Derrick*.

P. C. Boyle had come up through the oil fields with Gib. He came to Pithole in 1866 and went to work as a roustabout. After advancing to driller and then to oil scout, he gave up his job to enter journalism. He became editor of the *Derrick* in 1885. He also published a paper in Bradford, and in 1910 bought the *Oil Investor's Journal* and renamed it the *Oil and Gas Journal*. Boyle published numerous books on the oil industry and was at the time of Gib's death easily the world's leading publisher of petroleana.

Nor was Gib's book known to the editor of the Titusville *Herald*, who in his obituary remarked: "Stories as fabulous as ever were dreamed by frightened boy came to his lips readily in conversation and what he told would make a remarkable volume could they all be collected." The *Herald* article was copied by *Oil and Gas* without the addition of any reference to Gib's having published a book. Nor was Gib's book known to W. G. Long, who wrote of him in the *Oil and Gas Man's Magazine* in 1909.

I am convinced that if Gib's book had been published, copies would have been sent to the oil field press. If the manuscript was stolen and subsequently published, it was published so inconspicuously as to elude the searches of the library staffs and bibliographers who have aided me in my search.

GIB MORGAN AS ARTIST

 IF WE MAY JUDGE FROM THE TALES in Munn's *Useful Information*, the failure of this search is no great literary misfortune. For in spite of his effortless facility in the oral tale, Gib could not tell his stories effectively on paper. This rather than drunkenness probably accounts for any destruction of manuscripts he may have engaged in. It did not seem to occur to him that what he needed was a literal transcription of the oral forms. Like many another man with fresh materials to write about, he turned to traditional patterns of style: he looked for literary models. He found them in the long succession of newspaper humorists from John J. Hooper to Finley Peter Dunne, who pseudonymously expressed in ungrammatical and misspelled language their comments on the passing scene. But Gib Morgan was a teller of tales rather than a crackerbox philosopher and the devices of the newspaper humorists merely cluttered up his narrative.

A second fault is that he tried to put too much into the few pages that he wrote. Each oral tale was concerned with one specific adventure, either with a problem ingeniously solved or with a strange wonder witnessed. It was definitely separated from the preceding and succeeding tales by the comment and applause of the audience. It was told leisurely so that a man might relish it, and with sufficient circumstantial detail to arouse suspense and create the illusion of reality. In his written tales, on the other hand, Gib hurried from one marvel to the next without giving his reader time to enjoy any.

The superiority of Gib Morgan's oral tales over his written ones is not, however, due entirely to his lack of skill in writing. There are some advantages inherent in the oral medium itself. As long as he adhered to the spoken word, each tale was susceptible to infinite variation. "He never told a tale the same way twice," is a common remark among persons who have heard him. The yarn about striking a fine thing and then losing production by drilling just one more screw will serve as an example. Sometimes the thing struck would be whisky and the crew would go on a prolonged orgy of drunkenness until the well began to fail. Then they would rig up and drill just a little deeper only to strike a flow of horse stale which would drown out the liquor. Sometimes the valuable strike would be bay rum or eau de Cologne and the greed of Gib's employers would prompt them to have him drill deeper, always against his own judgment. The story of the piping of Big Toolie back to the States has its analogue in another story Gib told. Once a pipe line worker was teasing Gib about the worthlessness of drillers in general and of Gib in particular. Gib then told about an experience he had had with pipe liners. He was employed to lay a line along the Ohio. His ditch diggers were the poorest excuse for labor Gib had ever seen, but after months of coaxing and driving, he got the pipe line laid. Near Clarksburg there was a Y in the line, one prong leading into Pennsylvania and the other into West Virginia. The terminus was several hundred miles from the point where work had begun, and the shiftless men had not saved enough money to pay their way back home. They were not worth their fare and Gib refused to pay it. He did, however, offer to pipe them back through the new line. He carelessly put them in feet first and when they reached the Y, the right foot of each man went to West Virginia and the left foot went to Pennsylvania. "And that's the reason," said Gib, "there're so many half-men in the pipe line business."

This illustrates another characteristic of Gib's oral narratives. Their fluidity made it possible for him to adapt them to the immediate occasion and thus give them the appearance of spontaneity. More than one man has told me that he was present when Gib first "made up" this or that yarn. In 1907 when Gib was on his way to Oklahoma with a friend named Hood, they overheard some men on the train talking about their fine race horses. Gib sized them up as bookmakers looking for suckers and proceeded to tell about his famous reversible race horse twenty-two yards long. Hood thought that he had heard the horse invented, but there is evidence that Gib had created him earlier. Two informants give conflicting accounts of the origin of Gib's yarn about his big hotel. According to one, a young man had married the hotel owner's widow in a Pennsylvania town and was boasting about the excellence of the property he had thus acquired. Gib's remark was that the local hotel wasn't much. "You ought to see the hotel I built down at Beaumont. . . ." According to the other account a young man from the oil regions who had gone to the city for the first time, came back greatly impressed by the hotel at which he had stayed and became quite boresome in his efforts to impress others. Gib then told about his hotel, which he this time located in North Carolina. At this date nobody knows when Gib first told this or any other tale. He could so link a tale up with the circumstances of the moment that the hundredth telling sounded like the first.

Gib Morgan's tales are not so far removed from reality as they at first appear. If his lies were tall, the truth was also tall. From Drake's discovery in western Pennsylvania in 1859 to Dad Joiner's discovery in East Texas in 1930, the history of the oil industry is a succession of breath-taking wonders. Gib Morgan lived to see production in the United States advance from nothing to 18,317,-100 barrels annually. In 1930 it reached 100,713,300 barrels. At first the mysteriously black grease, whose exact properties varied from field to field, and from which chemists were continually fashioning new products, had to be pumped from the ground. Then in 1861 in certain locations along Oil creek wells were drilled from which it spouted of its own accord. How dangerous these wells were was tragically demonstrated by one of the first, which ignited and burned nineteen people to death. Before long it was discovered that oil was not confined to creek banks. New and marvelous records of production were established by individual wells. The Drake well yielded no more than eight barrels a day. The Little and Merrick on John Buchanan's farm at Rouseville came in in 1861 at three thousand. Numerous wells in the Pithole field produced between a thousand and two thousand. In the early nineties wells in the McDonald field exceeded two thousand barrels; and the Lucas gusher at Spindletop in 1901 produced 800,000 barrels of oil in nine days. No single well in East Texas exceeded the Lucas well in daily production, but by the middle of August, 1931, the field was yielding a million barrels of oil a day, and of course had ruined the market.

The statistics of the industry almost stagger the imagination. So do some of the traditional stories of success.

There were disappointments and failures and even suicides among the operators, but the public chose to forget them and to remember such incredible but true success stories as that of J. W. Sherman of Cleveland. In 1861 Sherman leased a part of James Foster's farm on Oil creek. Unable to buy an engine, he began "kicking" down a well by spring-pole and man power. This is the way J. J. McLaurin tells the story:

> His wife's money and his own played out before the second sand was penetrated. It was impossible to drill deeper by "hand power." A horse or an engine must be had to work the tools. "Pete," a white, angular equine, was procured for one-sixteenth interest in the well. The task becoming too heavy for "Pete," another sixteenth was traded to William Avery and J. E. Steele for a small engine and boiler. Lack of means to buy coal—an expensive article, sold only for "spot cash"—caused a week's delay. The owners of the well could not muster the "long green" to pay for one ton of fuel! For another sixteenth a purchaser grudgingly surrendered eighty dollars and a shot-gun! The last dollar had been expended when, on March sixteenth, 1862—just in season to celebrate St. Patrick's Day—the tools punctured the third sand. A crevice was hit, the tools were drawn out and in five minutes everything swam in oil. The Sherman well was flowing two-thousand barrels a day!

Sherman's experience was to be repeated many times. On January 10, 1901, Captain Lucas, the wildcatter of Spindletop, was ready to quit. He and his wife had burned most of their furniture to keep warm. They sat on chintz-covered boxes and ate from another box. This is the way a *Saturday Evening Post* writer dramatized the climactic event:

"I'm broke, wife; I'm penniless," slowly and sadly said Captain Lucas.

His wife, who had come down to cheer him and be with him in his big adventure, smiled bravely.

"Don't give up," she urged. "Drill just a little more—just a little more; maybe—"

"But I've put in my last dollar—out there—and I can't pay my men. Every foot from now on puts me further in debt. It wouldn't be right, wife. I'm going to quit."

Just then a strange roar came to them from across the prairie.

"Look!" cried Mrs. Lucas, who was the first to the window.

Lucas Number One was in. A solid stream of oil was gushing from a six-inch pipe a hundred and fifty feet into the air.

There were disappointed land owners, men who hoped for oil where it was not found, but they attracted less attention than those made rich by farms that had previously kept them poor. When one of John Blood's neighbors came into his money, he and his wife decided to take a trip to New York. Upon the advice of some wag who thought to play a practical joke on them, they went to the Astor House for lodging. They arrived each carrying a bundle tied up in a handkerchief. At the desk they demanded the best room in the whole shebang. When the clerk tried to direct them to another hotel, the citizens of Oil creek offered to buy the House, lock, stock and barrel. The clerk called the manager, who thought he would be safe in setting the price at a hundred thousand dollars. He was nonplussed when his guest pulled out his roll and counted out the currency on the spot. "Explanations followed, a parlor and bed room were assigned to the pair, and for days they were the lions of the metropolis."

More famous was Coal Oil Johnny Steele, who in most spectacular fashion spent a fortune of a half million dollars in two years. Once in Chicago Steele proposed that a benefit performance for Skill and Gaylord's minstrels be held in the Crosby Opera House. When the manager replied that he would not rent the house for a "nigger show," Steele counted out $200,000 and offered to buy him out. Upon sight of the money the owner relented and offered the hall free. The benefit was held, and the next day the owner received the finest carriage and team that could be found in

Chicago—a gift from Coal Oil Johnny. Through exploits like this Steele "called attention everywhere to the easy money-making possibilities in the oil region" and helped, thinks Paul Giddens, to promote the speculative boom in 1864-65.

As incredible as sudden rises from rags to riches was the manner in which some wells were located. Oil smellers, X-ray-eyed boys, water witches, clairvoyants, doodlebuggers found patrons and sometimes discovered oil. And so did dreamers. In 1864 a man by the name of Kepler, living at Hydetown, Pennsylvania, had a dream. He was in the woods with a young lady "who had been considered somewhat of a coquette." In their wanderings through the wood he suddenly noticed some distance away an Indian about to shoot him with a bow and arrow. The young lady handed him a rifle, which she had not had a moment before. He fired at the Indian, who immediately vanished. But from the spot where he had stood a river of oil gushed out. Some time later Kepler visited his brother's farm and on it recognized the scene of his dream. He marked the spot where the Indian had stood and the brothers interested some capitalists, Hyde and Egbert, who put down a well. The initial yield was 1500 barrels a day. Kepler supplemented his income by charging visitors a dime to see the wonder.

In 1908 Mrs. Weger of Crawford county, Illinois, was having a hard time. Her husband was dead and she was trying to support herself on an eighty-acre farm. She could not afford a hired hand, and she and the children had to do all the work. Most of it fell on her, for she sent the children to school when they had shoes and warm enough clothing. One night she dreamed she was sitting in a fine room in which there was a piano, upholstered furniture, and a Brussels carpet. She was making crochet, something she liked to do but never had leisure for. She dreamed the dream again. The third time she dreamed it, she, in her dream, got up and walked out of the house. Back of the henhouse she saw a strange contraption moving up and down. She had never seen an oil rig, but later when she did see one, she recognized it as the strange contraption of her dream. So when an operator offered to lease her land, she consented on condition that he write into the lease a clause permitting her to choose the location of the test well.

When the time came to drill, Cramer, the assistant production superintendent, sent the drilling contractor, O'Mara, down to drive the stake, telling him to ask Mrs. Weger where to drive it. The

51

farm was divided into eight ten-acre tracts, and if the test brought oil, a well was to be drilled on each. When the drilling contractor arrived at the farm, Mrs. Weger was not there. Instead of hunting her up, he drove the stake on one of the corner blocks, got in his buggy and drove back to town, about twelve miles. There he told the assistant superintendent what he had done.

Cramer insisted that the contract must be observed to the letter. They went back and found Mrs. Weger and told her to pick the location. She chose the spot back of the henhouse where she had seen the contraption in her dream. The well was a good producer. On six of the remaining tracts good wells were also brought in. But the eighth well to be dug, the one on the location O'Mara had made, was dry. If this had been the first well drilled, the lease would have been abandoned and Mrs. Weger would not have got her fine room, her piano, and her upholstered furniture. Nor would she have had time to sit in her chair and make crochet while her children were at school.

Nor were all self-drilling wells creations of Gib Morgan's imagination. A well was brought in on Jacob Mildren's farm in Pennsylvania in April of 1870. Before tubing could be set, the derrick burned to the ground. "The tools are still in the well," reported the Oil City *Times* on May 3, "and the occasional flow of gas raises them a number of feet, when they fall back with great force, each time increasing the depth of the hole. By this process the well has drilled itself upwards of fifty feet within the past two weeks." Before the tools were finally recovered in June, they had gone down another fifty feet.

Fully as remarkable was the Seneca Oil Company's gusher in the Chipmunk field near Bradford. When this well blew in on May 27, 1898, the oil was ignited by the boiler fire and the crew ran for their lives. On the next day the well drilled itself through the oil sand and struck a flow of salt water, which put out the fire. Three days later the water was cased off and the well was producing twenty barrels of oil an hour.

There were freakish incidents in drilling too, some almost as fantastic as Gib Morgan's tales. If an article in the New York *Herald* is to be trusted, not all the whisky wells existed in Gib's imagination. As the event was reported, a well in southeastern Oklahoma was being drilled on top of a hill. At about two hundred feet "the drill seemed to fall into a cavity" and fumes of whisky came to the surface. The driller drew out the tools, emptied his lunch bucket and lowered it on the bailer line. It came up, he was reported to have said, full of the "best corn whisky I ever had laid my lip to." The explanation was that he had drilled into a barrel of liquor in a moonshiner's cave.

It might be said of Gib Morgan, then, that he distorted the truth in the interest of art. His object, however, was not belief, but skepticism. The satiric intent of many of his tales is obvious.

Because so many incredible things did happen in the oil fields, there was predisposition toward belief in the marvelous. Even the Oil City *Derrick*, which always maintained high standards of accuracy, seems to have been taken in occasionally. In 1877 it published an account of a well near Millerstown that produced "absolutely refined oil," which when put into a lamp burned "with a brilliant, clear flame, and without any more deposit on the wick than results from ordinary kerosene." The story runs true to the folk pattern. The well was supposed to be dry and the producer was about to abandon it. "Before doing so, however, he concluded to go a little deeper and was rewarded by finding this wonderful exhibition of nature's skill in manufacturing refined oil." It would seem that somebody had salted a well with kerosene.

He was not the only man to take advantage of the current predisposition to belief. Fly-by-the-night oil companies issued brochures that needed only slight exaggeration to become first-rate tall tales. Others besides Gib Morgan saw the possibilities of humor in this literature. The *Typographical Advertiser* for January, 1865, carried the following burlesque announcement:

Antipodal Petroleum Company, capital stock, $1,000,000,-000; shares, par value, $10,000 each. Price $25. The well is drilled entirely through the earth extending from Oil creek, Pa., to Hoang Ho, in the Celestial Empire, and consequently has a double outlet. An immense blow pipe will be inserted in the Chinese outlet to promote an unbroken flow of oil from the western well, which, it is supposed, will equal to 100 barrels of refined petroleum per minute. Particular Phitts, Esq., Treasurer, and Hon. Gointoem Strong, President.

A more elaborate burlesque prospectus appeared in the Boston *Commercial* about the same time. The company, named the Munchausen Philosopher's Stone and Gull Creek Grand Consolidated Oil Company, was capitalized at $4,000,000,000, and had a working capital of $37.50. The president was S. W. Indle, the vice-president Hon. R. Ascal, and treasurer D. Faulter. Among the directors were Lemuel Gulliver and Baron Munchausen. The company possessed vast holdings, including the Munchausen tract upon which wells produced, among other things, cooking butter, XXX Ale, cod liver oil, quinine, sardines, and the milk of human kindness.

On the Ananias and Sapphira Tract the company had not been so fortunate. They had struck a vein of lawyers.

This was an unfortunate strike and far from profitable. They claimed that, as they were a part of the land, they had a fee in it. Our learned legal adviser contended, upon trial, that as they had not been in possession of the surface or soil for twenty-one years, they had no title; and further, that as the vein immediately under them was brimstone, it was evident that they were more than half way down, and should go to the other side. The judge in this case decided in favor of both parties and advised a compromise. This was done in the usual manner. The attorneys of the company took five-ninths and the other side took five-ninths, leaving the balance of the property to the company.

That Gib Morgan used his tales to satirize individuals of whom he disapproved has already been suggested. A striking example is furnished by his rebuke to a pipe line foreman near Cherry Grove, Pennsylvania, in 1882. Gib was among a group of men hired to clear and grade a piece of ground upon which storage tanks were to be erected. The foreman, a man named McQuay, was known as a relentless driver of labor, who enjoyed being known as a tough and explosive character. One day as the crew was eating lunch, McQuay asserted that he had once killed a workman who would not perform satisfactorily.

Gib listened to the story and then said solemnly, "I never killed a man, but I came very near it one time." Then he launched into the tale of his fight with a Negro. After that McQuay's boasts and threats brought only laughter.

Perhaps Long's comparison of Gib Morgan with Mark Twain is based on this kind of satire. One is able to point out a close and specific parallel.

In 1880 Mark Twain found in the New York *Post* a dispatch

reprinted from the San Francisco *Call*, which told of the discovery of gold-bearing waters at Calistoga. The discoverer had extracted gold valued at $1,060 from ten barrels of water. Mark Twain wrote the *Post* that he himself had once owned those springs and that he had extracted gold by filling his uncle with the water, allowing him to stand fifteen minutes, and then inserting him in an "exhausted receiver, which had the effect of sucking gold out through the pores. I have often taken more than $11,000 out of that old man in a day and a half."

But the spring did not compare with the gold-bearing air of Catgut Canyon, from which the metal was precipitated by "contact with human flesh in a state of passion. The time that William Abrahams was disappointed in love he used to step out doors when the wind was blowing, and come in again and begin to sigh and sigh, and his brother and I would extract over $1.50 out of every pore."

In 1877 there appeared in the Oil City *Derrick* the following article:

Lockport (N. Y.) Times, May 14.

Something less than a year ago Dr. L. W. Bristol, the well known dentist of this city, came to the conclusion that an accelerating condition of poor health by which he was afflicted was occasioned by a tape worm. Being scientific as well as self-reliant, he proceeded to study up on the tape worm business, and when he had learned all he could on that subject, he proceeded to treat himself. The result was that in August, 1876, he passed a tape worm measuring thirty-two feet in length. Some two months after this the same symptoms again reappeared, and, after the same treatment, he succeeded in bringing away fourteen feet, which he found did not have the neck and head, and in two months thereafter, being about May 1st, by the same treatment previously pursued, he brought away the balance of the last tape worm, measuring sixteen feet—making a total of eighty-two feet of tape worms since last August. These tape worms have all been preserved in alcohol by Dr. Bristol and can be seen by the curious at this office.

There are some facts in connection with Dr. Bristol's experience in this matter that are of great value to the public. When convinced that he was troubled with tape worms he commenced the study of the subject, and, as the result of such study, he treated himself, and so successfully that all these pests have been removed without any sickness or pain, and the doctor claims that he would sooner remove a tape worm than have a bad cold any time. But what is more startling, if correct, is the theory which Dr. Bristol has come to in regard to tape worms as the result of his experience. He is of the opinion that the germ of these worms was received from a dog while he was in a hunting camp many years ago, in Canada, and that he suffered many years from them without knowing what was the matter. Two companions who were with him in that camp—the late Daniel Winer and James C. Bacon—died from troubles similar to those which have afflicted Dr. Bristol, and which baffled all medical aid. Dr. Bristol is now sincerely of the opinion that they died from tape worms. However this may be, his experience in this matter is of great practical interest and should become generally known.

If Gib Morgan wrote a letter to the *Derrick*, it wasn't published. But he did put into oral circulation a tale that has had a wider audience than the *Derrick* would have given it, a tale that suffers nothing in comparison with Mark Twain's letter to the *Post*.

The Tales Gib Morgan Told

WHEN THE OIL EXCITEMENT BROKE out in West Virginia, Gib was employed by the Scarcely Able and Hardly Ever Get Oil Company (capitalized at $5,000,000,000.00, with a paid capital of $300.00) to go into the region and lease and drill on everything in sight. Gib had a lot of surprises waiting for him down there.

He thought he had seen hills in Clarion and Venango counties back in Pennsylvania, but by the time he got to Wheeling he realized that he hadn't known what a hill was. At the place where he boarded while drilling the first well, he could look up the chimney and see the cows come home, and the only way he could

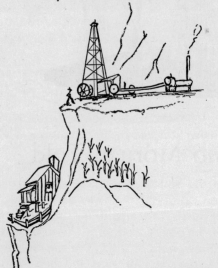

grease a wagon was to chain it to a stump. He drove the stake for the first location in the edge of a corn patch because that was the only place where he could find a piece of level ground big enough to set up the rig on. From the top of the derrick he could look down the chimney and see the farmer's wife churning.

Gib got the rig up the first day, but as it was about dusk by the time he had everything in place, he decided to wait until the next morning to spud in. As he had driven out that morning he had seen a good many hogs along the trail, eating acorns and rooting in the underbrush. And he had noticed that every hog he got a good look at had a round hole in his right ear. He supposed that this was the owner's mark, and a good mark it was too, since it would be a hard one to change.

Gib had his tool dresser hitch up the team, and since he was going to take the short steep way down rather than the long winding way up, he locked the back wheels to brake the buckboard as he drove down to the farm house. Just as Gib was about to get in to drive off, up came a drove of hogs, thousands of hogs, big hogs, little hogs, and spotted hogs. On the brink of the mountain they stopped short. Every hog sat down and put his right hind leg through the hole in his right ear to rough-lock himself down the side of the mountain. One would have thought that an avalanche or an earthquake had visited the country by the noise they made going down. Hundreds of tons of stone and gravel followed them to the bottom.

As he watched them he discovered that they belonged to many different owners, for about half way down the mountain, the big stream of hogs began to divide into smaller streams, each flowing to a different farm house below.

Gib later talked to the natives about what he had seen, and they told him that their grandfathers had had to cut holes in their hogs' ears, but that after several generations of careful breeding, the hole had become a hereditary trait, and now a pig with a solid ear was as rare a throw-back as one having a short snout and short legs.

⌐ HOW GIB PAID A BOARD BILL

IN THAT SAME REGION THERE WAS one farmer whose hogs had been attacked by an eye disease, and every brute of them except an old sow had lost its eyesight. He trained this old sow to take care of the rest of the drove. They could root around the bushes and find mast and keep as fat as the neighbors' hogs, but they never could find their way back to water without help. When they got thirsty, they would line up, each hog taking in its mouth the tail of the hog in front of it. Then the one at the head of the line would take hold of the tail of the old sow and she would lead them first to the creek for water and then home.

Now before Gib had completed his first well, his money got low and he saw it was going to run out entirely before he got paid off. He asked the farmer he was staying with whether he would be willing to accept hogs in place of cash for his board bill. The farmer said they weren't used to much money up in that neck of the woods anyway, that they generally paid their bills in pumpkins or corn or hogs or whisky, and if Gib wanted to pay in hogs that would suit him fine.

So the next day about dusk, when the hogs always went to water, Gib was down at the creek with a sharp knife in his pocket. Pretty soon here came the old sow with twenty shoats following her. Gib waited until they had finished drinking and formed the line again. Then he slipped up quietly and took the old sow's tail in his left hand and cut it off with his right. Still holding the tail, he led the whole drove home.

↜ HOW GIB SAVED A FARMER'S LIFE

GIB HAD SOME BAD LUCK ON THAT first well, which turned out to be the good luck of the farmer. About five hundred feet down he broke a pin and lost his bit. The only thing to do was to rig up a string of fishing tools and go to work. He put a pair of long stroke jars below the drill stem and below the jars a horn socket. The horn socket was a tube with a conical flare at the bottom to fit over the broken bit and a spring latch to hold the bit as it was being drawn from the well.

As Gib was making up the string of tools he noticed the farmer out hoeing corn. At the end of each row he would stop and lean on his hoe and rest a while before he hoed the next row. Just as Gib was about to lower the tools into the well, he heard a loud crack like a stick breaking and saw a cloud of dust coming from the edge of the field. At first he thought it was a hog going down the hill, but pretty soon he heard yelling and cussing, and a boy hollered out, "Ma, ma, Pa's done fell out of the corn patch."

Gib knew that something had to be done and done quick. He threw the tools off the ledge and let out cable. When he had run out about fifteen hundred feet, he caught the old man's head with the horn socket and reeled him back up.

That night the old lady said, "Jim, I told you you ought to build a fence around that there corn patch. It's dangerous to work up there."

Jim said, "It warn't a fence I needed. It war a new hoe handle. I knowed that old one war a-gittin' weak."

The old man and the old lady surely were grateful to Gib for saving his life. After that nothing they had was too good for him.

↜ HOW GIB NEARLY GOT A BIT

WHEN GIB GOT THE BIT OUT, IT was so badly broken that he couldn't use it any more, and the

Hardly Able and Scarcely Ever Git hadn't provided him with an extra. There wasn't anything to do but to shut down and go to Mannington for a new one. It was a long trip and he hated to lose the time, but it had to be done, and he thought he had just as well start that afternoon and camp on the way. So he and his tool dresser got in the buckboard and started out. The Hardly Able was having lots of competition now, for there was a rig on every hill.

As they were driving along down the valley at a good brisk trot, Gib thought he noticed something lying out in the bushes that wasn't a log.

"Do you see what I see over there?" he asked the tool dresser. "What does that look like to you?"

"It looks like a bit to me," said the tool dresser.

"That's what it looks like to me too," said Gib.

They got out and looked. Sure enough there was a good twelve-inch bit, nearly new, just like the one they had broken.

"Looks like we won't have to go any further," said Gib. "Take a hold and let's load it in."

But just as they were about to lay hands on the bit, a fishing tool ran out and grabbed it. They watched it run up the hillside and disappear into a hole. Then on top of the hill they saw a derrick that they hadn't noticed before.

〜 HOW GIB GOT A BIT

ABOUT DARK THEY MADE CAMP and cooked and ate their supper; and while they sat around the fire and smoked their pipes, they suddenly heard a great splashing in the creek about a hundred yards from camp. The toolie said it sounded to him like a coon slapping sun fish out of the water. Gib, who had been a great hunter back in Venango and Clarion counties, wasn't so sure. He said if it was a coon it was the biggest coon in seven states. He said it sounded to him like a whole precinct of coons holding their annual convention and fish fry.

Anyhow, they decided to take their lantern and walk down to where the noise was. What they found was a cable coming out of a hole in the side of a mountain and a string of cable tools drilling in the creek bed. Gib remembered what had happened further up the valley, and this time he wasn't going to take any chances. He ran back and got a crowbar he always carried in the buckboard and stuck it through the jars. Then he told the toolie to go back and get the tongs, and not to spare the horses either. Before daylight they had the bit on their own string of tools and were drilling again.

It surely was lucky that he had that crowbar. His toolie hadn't more than got started back when the driller up on the hill started trying to pull his tools.

⤸ GIB AS OPERATOR

GIB WOULD SAY ONE THING FOR the mountain people of West Virginia: they might be suspicious of a stranger at first, but once you made friends with them, they were the most loyal people on earth. He remembered one man in particular to whom he took a liking. He gave him a job as tool dresser and taught him to drill.

After Gib had completed a couple of wells in the West Virginia field, he decided to go into the oil business for himself. He didn't have much money, but he had seen men get rich on less. The first thing he did was to get up a block of leases. Then he began to sell interests in order to get capital to put down a well.

He had all sorts of trouble from the beginning. He hadn't got down very far when the hole caved and had to be cased. Then it wasn't long until it had to be cased again. He had to sell more interests to buy casing. Then he struck a hard slanting formation and got a crooked hole. It took two weeks' work with a side reamer to straighten it up. He had to sell more interests to meet his payroll. He lost his tools and had expensive fishing jobs and had to sell still more interests.

He'd been so busy that he hadn't had much time for book-keeping, but one day he got out his pencil and began figuring, adding up all the interests he had sold. They came to a hundred and fifty percent. Gib thought it over and decided he'd better leave the country for a while. He left between sundown and sunup. He went to the South Sea Islands, to Russia, to South America and to many other places where he had many remarkable adventures, and when he finally came back to the United States, his venture in oil promotion seemed to have been forgotten. In fact he had forgotten it himself.

Then one time, fully fifty years after he had first got up the block of leases, he went into the hill country of West Virginia fishing. One day as he was following a stream upward, he kept thinking that the scenery looked familiar, but he couldn't be sure whether he had ever seen it before or not.

After a while he came in sight of an oil derrick. There was a fire under the boiler and the walking beam was moving up and down. He supposed he was approaching a new wildcat, and he was afraid he might be mistaken for an oil scout. But he walked on toward the rig. Sitting on the driller's seat was an old man with white whiskers reaching down to his waist. He jumped down from the stool, ran and met Gib and hugged him. "Hello, Gib," he said in a squeaky voice. "I knowed you'd come back. After five years my toolie quit me. Said you wasn't coming back. But I knowed you'd come."

Then Gib remembered that in his hurry to get away he had forgotten to tell the driller on tour to knock off.

⌐ HOW GIB DRILLED ON PIKE'S PEAK

THE ONLY OTHER PLACE WHERE Gib ever drilled in country as perpendicular as West Virginia was in Colorado. He was then working for Standard Oil of New Jersey. Their head geologist had located a well just by making a cross on the map, and Gib was sent to drill it. When he got out there, he found that the rockhound had put that cross right smack dab on top of Pike's Peak. The crew wanted to set up down in a valley somewhere. They said the brass hats back in New Jersey wouldn't know the difference anyway. But Gib said no. He hadn't seen a location he couldn't drill on yet, and he wasn't going to be stumped at his age. So they snaked the timbers up and built a derrick on top of Pike's Peak. But when they got the rig up, there wasn't any room for the engine and boiler. The nearest piece of level ground big enough to put them on was twenty-three miles below. It took forty-six miles of belting to connect the power plant, and a belt that long will stretch a good deal. They had to relace it every few days to take up the slack. Gib saved all the pieces they cut off and had enough leather to keep his boots half soled for the rest of his life.

It was too far to walk from the engine to the rig, so Gib bought a mountain mule to ride back and forth. At first he was a little bit leary about riding the mule down, but the natives said there wasn't any danger. All the mules in that country were used to mountains. They were sure footed and never stumbled. Thus assured, Gib got on the critter to ride him down to the engine. As he rode he could see the mule's head between the stirrups.

When he got about half way down he felt something warm on the back of his neck. He ran his hand under his overcoat collar and when he drew it back it didn't smell like Hoyt's Cologne. He decided that while the mule might be safe enough, he would prefer to get about some other way. He sold the brute, and after that when he wanted to go from the engine to the rig or from the rig to the engine, he just threw his saddle on the belt and rode it up or down.

ᐦ GIB ON A TEXAS RANCH

GIB DRILLED THE FIRST OIL WELL on the plains of West Texas, but he didn't discover a field. The well was a duster, but Gib always maintained that if the brass hats had let him go on down he would have found oil. They sent him down there to make a test and he proposed to make a test. But after he had drilled eight years, they made him abandon the hole. They said that if he did bring in a well it would be in China, and they didn't have any leases there. Some English syndicate would get the production. So they told Gib to plug up the hole and come on back and get ready to go to South America.

Now Gib had heard the cattle baron who owned the land talk about buying some of this new barbed wire and fencing off a little calf pasture of a couple of million acres, but his cowboys wouldn't dig the postholes because they couldn't figure out any way to do it on horseback. So Gib just pulled up the well, which was a lot

64

easier than plugging it anyway, and they sawed it into eighteen-inch sections and used it for postholes.

The cattle baron was so grateful to Gib that he wouldn't take any money for board, although Gib had been living with him for eight years. Gib insisted on paying him, but he said no, he was always glad to have good company at his ranch, and besides Gib had saved him thousands of dollars on postholes. Gib asked him if there wasn't something he could do to sort of help out around the place, and the rancher said well if it would make him feel any better he might go out and nail up some barbed wire. So the next morning Gib took a hatchet and a boot leg full of staples and started out. It was a pretty day and the work was interesting, and before Gib realized it the sun was about to set. He started walking along the fence toward the ranch house. The pasture was so big that it took him two days to get back.

⤳ GIB'S BIGGEST RIG

ANOTHER TIME HE WAS IN TEXAS he had better luck. It was fitting, Gib thought, though only a coincidence, that the biggest oil rig ever built should be built in the biggest state in the union. It all came about like this.

There was a certain region down in Texas where the Standard rockhounds figured that there was oil under the ground, but they hadn't been able to get to it. They had sent their crack drilling crews and production men down, but the formation above the oil sand was so cavy that they hadn't been able to make a hole. They would start with a twenty-four-inch bit and case with a twenty-two-inch casing. Then they would make a few more feet of hole and would have to set a twenty-inch casing. They would cut a little more ditch and then they would have to case again. And it would go on like that until the casing became too small for the tools to go through, and after all that expense they would have to abandon the hole.

Finally John D. himself called Gib in and showed him the logs of all the wells they had tried to make, and said, "Gib, do you think you can make me a hole down to the oil sand?"

Gib looked at the logs a while and then he said, "John D., if you'll put up the money, I'll put down the hole."

"It's a deal," said John D., and they shook hands on it, but they didn't drink, both being temperance men.

65

First Gib went over to Pittsburgh to see the Oil Well Supply Company and told them how to make the special tools he wanted, some big tools and some little tools. Then he went to Texas and started putting up the rig.

The derrick covered an acre of ground, and since Gib expected to be there for some time he fixed it up nice. He weatherboarded it on the outside and plastered it on the inside. It was so high that he had it hinged in two places so that he could fold it back to let the moon get by. It took a tool dresser fourteen days to climb to the top to grease the crown pulleys. That is the reason Gib had to hire thirty tool dressers. At any time there would be fourteen going up, fourteen coming down, one on the top and one on the ground. A day's climbing apart he built bunk houses for the men to sleep in. These bunk houses had hot and cold showers and all the modern conveniences.

By the time the derrick was up, the tools began to arrive from Pittsburgh. The biggest string of tools reached to within ten feet of the crown block. The drill stem was twelve feet in diameter. At the first indication of caving Gib cased the well with thousand-barrel oil tanks riveted together. This reducted the hole to twenty feet. He put on an eighteen-foot bit and made about fifty feet of hole before he had to case again. Down about five hundred feet he had to go to a smaller bit, one about six feet in diameter. At a thousand feet he was using standard tools. At two thousand feet he was using his specially made small tools and casing with one-inch tubing. But he hadn't figured it quite fine enough, for he hadn't got the oil sand when the smallest drill he had wouldn't go through the tubing. But that didn't stump Gib. He brought in the well with a needle and thread.

↳ THE BUTTERMILK SAND

Some of Gib's most remarkable adventures took place in the Fiji Islands, where he was sent by a British syndicate to drill for essence of peppermint, which was expected at a depth of nine thousand feet. If he failed to get a paying well at that depth, he was to drill on into a lower sand for bay rum, which was expected at a depth of twelve thousand feet.

He set up his rig on one of the smaller islands, spudded in, and

66

soon had the drilling under way. The going was easy and he had a good deal of leisure time on his hands. He knocked around on the island a good deal looking for companionship, but he didn't find the natives very sociable, and they couldn't speak United States anyway. Finally he got so bored that he felt he had to get away for a day or two, and as the work was coming along fine, he thought it wouldn't hurt to leave his crew to carry on while he visited the port on one of the larger islands. There he met the Noble, Grand, Worshipful, Master, Chanceller, Commander, Exalted Ruler and Jibbonancy of the Islands. This potentate, who spoke Oxford, gave Gib the keys to his spacious grass and palm-leaf mansion and entertained him so royally that he forgot all about the well for a whole week.

When he got back to the location, drilling had stopped. The men were sitting around under palm trees, slick and fat and too lazy to move. They had struck a flow of buttermilk soon after Gib left, and they had done nothing the whole time he was gone but sit around and drink buttermilk and sleep.

⤙ THE CHAMPAGNE SAND

GIB GOT THEM TOGETHER AND MADE them case off the buttermilk. They went back to work and soon were making hole right along. Then after a couple of weeks a messenger came in a canoe, bringing an invitation from the Noble, Grand, Worshipful Master, Chancellor, Commander, Exalted Ruler and Jibbonancy for Gib to visit him again. He said he had planned a big party and he hoped Gib would not disappoint him. Now Gib had never been presented at the Court of St. James's as some of his old neighbors back in Venango county had, but he knew enough to know that an invitation from royalty was the same as a command. He told the crew to stay at work come hell or high water, and then he set out for the royal palace.

He had an even better time than he had had on his first visit, and before he knew it, he had stayed two weeks. When he got back the walking beam was still and the boiler was cold. The men were raising so much hell that he could hear them whooping it up while he was still five miles at sea. They had struck a flow of champagne.

Gib tried to case this off as he had done the buttermilk, but he never could get the crew sober enough to work. In fact he was the only white man on the island sober enough to walk straight, and he couldn't set a casing by himself. Besides, the sight of these drunken brutes was so disgusting that he couldn't stand to look at them. He just got in his launch and went off and left them there, and so far as he knew they were there yet, still drunk as lords.

All of which shows what liquor will do for a man if he fools with it long enough.

ᕽ BIG TOOLIE

GIB CABLED FOR A NEW RIG AND crew. He said he wanted some real drillers and tool dressers this time, not a bunch of oil field bums. They arrived on the next ship and Gib set up on another island where the geology indicated that the bay rum was above the buttermilk and champagne sands.

All the new crew looked like good men, but one of the new tool dressers was an especially fine big fellow, twenty-eight inches between the eyes and so tall that he could grease the crown pulleys without taking a foot off the ground. He did not say what his name was, and Gib was too polite to ask him, so he just called him Big Toolie. Big Toolie was a good-natured, playful giant who liked his little tricks. Sometimes when Gib would be on the

driller's stool, Big Toolie would sneak around and put his foot on the walking beam and either stall the engine or throw the belt off. But he was a good hand and a likeable cuss, and Gib put up with his jokes for a good while. He saw, however, that he would have to find a way to break him. He told him to keep the steam gauge at a hundred and twenty-five pounds. He kept a close watch on him, and one day when Big Toolie was about to step on the walking beam, Gib gave the engine all it had. The beam threw Big Toolie over the derrick and he landed in the slush pit on his head. He crawled out and walked up to Gib and stuck out his hand and said, "Mr. Morgan, I'm your man from now on."

⌐ HOW GIB LOST A FORTUNE

THE DRILLING WENT ON FINE. GIB pulled the tools one day when he was down about fifteen hundred feet and found them covered with a whitish liquid.

"There's the buttermilk again," he said to Big Toolie. "Get busy and let's case it off before the other tour finds out about it."

But Gib was tired and thirsty and the buttermilk looked so good that he just had to have a drink of it. He stabbed the bailer into the well and brought up a bucketful. It wasn't buttermilk; it was sweet cream. Still he thought he had better case it off.

While Big Toolie was fixing up the seed bag, Gib had an idea.

"Big Toolie," he asked, "do you suppose these heathens ever heard of ice cream?"

"I don't know," said Big Toolie, "but if they ever tasted it once they never would be able to get enough."

"That's what I was thinking," said Gib.

He got the crew together and told them to install a pump, and he took the first boat for the United States. He bought the biggest and best ice cream factory he could find, pasteurizers, refrigerating machines—everything—and shipped it back with men to operate it. It took every cent he had, but he finally got it up and was ready to begin production. He turned on the steam and started the pump.

Then he discovered that all his fine machinery was useless. While he was gone the cream had soured. And that is the way Gib lost his fortune.

⌐ HOW GIB LOST FAVOR WITH
THE EXALTED RULER

THEY CASED OFF THE SOUR CREAM and started drilling again. They worked so hard that Gib decided that they had earned a holiday. At nine thousand feet they shut down one Saturday to rest over Sunday. They pulled the tools so they wouldn't get stuck and hung them to one side of the derrick, threw some boards over the hole, and went to their boarding house to dream of a flowing well, for they were nearing the long looked-for bay rum sand.

When they started up on Monday morning the tools stopped at two hundred feet from the bottom of the hole. They wondered what this could mean. They had had no cave.

69

They hitched on and commenced to drill. When they had let out about twenty feet of cable, they pulled the tools and ran the bailer.

What a sight!

One of the men cried out, "We've struck the jugular vein of the earth. It's blood."

"Not so fast, brother," said Gib. "We've struck the old devil square on the head. You'll find a lot of hair mixed in with the blood."

"And bones," cried Big Toolie.

While they were examining the contents of the bailer, the Noble, Grand, Worshipful Master, Chancellor, Commander, Exalted Ruler and Jibbonancy came along mad as the devil.

He said that in the eyes of his people they were all low down murderers, for they had killed all the monkeys on the island, and that the monkey was a sacred animal. He said that on Sunday the monkeys had gathered at the well to hold a convention in the derrick. One of their numbers had accidentally fallen into the well. Monkeys, he said, were better Christians than white men, for when one monkey was in distress all the others would go to his rescue. They had formed a chain down into the well to try to reach their fallen comrade, but the one on top had lost his hold and all had perished.

Since Gib had been a guest of the Exalted Ruler, he wouldn't have them beheaded, but if they stayed around he wouldn't be responsible for what his people might do.

They spent the rest of the day dismantling the rig and moving it to an island that had a different Exalted Ruler.

᠆ HOW GIB SOLVED THE FUEL PROBLEM

ON THE NEW LOCATION THEY GOT along fine at first. Then they began to have trouble. The island was small and had little growing upon it except cocoanut palms. When they got down about five thousand feet they had burned up all the firewood. There wasn't anything to do except fire the boiler with cocoanuts. They kept up the steam better than wood, but as they exploded as soon as they got hot, they kept up a continuous noise like musketry in battle, which began to get on the nerves of some of the crew. Gib solved the problem by moving the boiler a mile back from the rig and furnishing horses for the tool dressers.

70

AT SIX THOUSAND FEET THE TOOLS got stuck and in trying to pull them out, they broke the cable. In their hurry to get away from the island of the dead monkeys, they had forgotten their horn socket, and they were afraid to go back for it. It looked as though they were going to have to shut down until they could get one from the United States. Then Gib remembered that he had seen a lighthouse on a promentory at the south end of the island. He went over and borrowed the fog horn, screwed it on a singer, and using it for a horn socket, fished out the tools.

He bailed out, dressed the bit, and started drilling. He had not made more than a couple of screws when the tools stuck again. Now the bailer had gone down easy enough, and Gib was stumped for a while in trying to figure out what the trouble could be. He went to the pit to examine the slush. It smelled kind of peculiar and he tasted it. Then he knew what had happened. He had struck a vein of alum and it had shrunk the hole.

Now Gib knew that there was a big rum distillery on the island, but having no interest in that sort of thing he had never paid any attention to it. But now he saw that there might be some justification for liquor after all. He went over and bought forty barrels of rum. When the wagons drove up, the crew all got happy, for they thought that at last Gib had overcome his aversion to liquor and was going to throw a big party. They knocked out a bung and started drinking before Gib could stop them. Big Toolie picked the barrel up by the chines and drank from the bunghole. They were having such a good time that Gib did not have the heart to stop them. He told them to help themselves.

When they got so drunk that they did not know what he was doing, Gib poured all the rum they had left into the well. It neutralized the alum until he could drill through the formation and set a casing.

⌐ ONE SCREW TOO MANY

AS GIB WENT ON DOWN WITH THE well, his corns got to hurting him, and he knew from past experience that when his corns hurt him he was about to strike something big. The further down he went the more his corns hurt, and when he approached twelve thousand feet, they tortured him so that he couldn't stand still. He drove his crew until he was ashamed of himself, but he just had to hurry up and finish that well and get his misery over with.

Then one day after he had run the bailer and measured the sand line at 1195 feet, and had run the tools down and drilled for about a half an hour, he heard the loudest roaring and rumbling he had ever heard in an oil well. He knew he had a gusher sure enough. He got the tools out and set the Christmas tree on the casing head before the flow got to the top. He got the well to flowing into the storage without losing a drop. In an hour it had filled a two-thousand-barrel tank—the prettiest, clearest, and sweetest smelling bay rum you ever saw.

If the brass hats had only let him alone, the well would have made billions. But the big boys are never satisfied. If you get them a five-thousand-barrel well, they want ten thousand barrels; if you get them twenty-five thousand, they want fifty thousand. One of the big production men got to the island and arrived at the well just as the storage tank was full. He told Gib to run the tools back in and drill just one more screw.

Then the thing happened that Gib had warned him about. The drill went through the bay rum horizon and the whole field was drowned out.

It wasn't salt water. It was an unmentionable liquid that brought back memories of his boyhood days when he worked in a livery stable.

↬ HOW GIB LAID A PIPE LINE
UNDER THE OCEAN

GIB DRILLED ON OTHER ISLANDS BUT he never did strike another vein of bay rum. However, he got plenty of oil—so much in fact that he had to take time out and lay a seventy-two-inch line under the Pacific Ocean back to the United States. After some experimentation in metallurgy, Gib developed a pipe flexible enough to be wound on huge spools and unreeled from the back of a ship. The line was to run straight to Los Angeles and from there to St. Louis, where it would fork, one branch to go to New York and the other to Chicago. He had ships full of pipe anchored all the way from Fiji to Los Angeles. First he put up a pumping station. He told the pumper to give him an hour and then turn on the pumps. Gib beat the oil to Los Angeles by an hour and ten minutes.

↜ THE END OF BIG TOOLIE

HE THEN WENT BACK TO DRILL OUT the leases, putting down a well for every ten acres. Before he got them drilled, Big Toolie got word that his woman was about to marry another man. Big Toolie loaded his six-shooter and went down to the port to catch the next steamer. But when she came in she was already loaded to the gunwales, and the captain said that if they took Big Toolie on, they would be sure to founder before they got a hundred miles at sea.

Big Toolie was so cut up that all he did was to sit around and mope and finger his six-shooter. Since he wasn't any good as a tool dresser any more, Gib told him he would get him home faster than he could go on any ship that ever crossed the ocean.

"How can you do it?" Big Toolie asked.

"Don't you remember that big pipe line we laid?" asked Gib.

"That's right," said Big Toolie. "Put me in it."

So Gib fixed him up a gallon of rum and a basket of grub and put him in the pipe line and started the pump. Everything would have been fine if in the excitement of getting him off Gib hadn't got a little careless and put him in feet first. He went through as slick as grease until he got to the Y at St. Louis. There his right foot started to New York and left foot to Chicago, and that was the last of the best tool dresser that Gib Morgan ever had.

Still, there was some consolation. He never lived to know that his woman married the other man.

↜ A NIGHT IN THE JUNGLE

GIB HAD HARDLY GOT BACK TO THE United States from the Fiji Islands when Standard Oil of New Jersey hired him to go down to South America and put down some wells. It was wildcat territory down there, and they didn't know what was under the ground, but they said they were in the oil

73

business and if he struck anything else like bay rum or Hoyt's Eau de Cologne, he was to case it off and go on after the oil. They thought it wouldn't be over ten thousand feet to the oil sand if there was any.

Gib disobeyed his orders just a little bit, but if he hadn't, he never would have got down to the oil.

When he got to the first location, he found that they had driven the green stake right out in the middle of a jungle. They had put up a bunkhouse, but they hadn't screened it, and as it turned out screens would have done no good anyway. The first night the mosquitoes were so bad that Gib and his crew couldn't sleep. They built a smudge and tried to smoke the critters out, but it did more harm than good. For they saw the smoke and came from miles away just to see what it was, and when they got there they went to work on Gib and his crew. All the men were grumbling and threatening to leave, and Gib felt like throwing up the job himself. But he never had quit a job and he didn't want to start it now.

He began looking around for an idea. Then he thought of the two thirty-thousand-barrel oil tanks they had brought along for storage. He got the crew together and went to work setting one of them up. They didn't bother about the bottom. They just riveted the walls together and put the roof on. Then they got in it. Presently they began to hear something that sounded like musket balls glancing off the steel walls of the tank.

"Storms come up mighty quick down here," said the tool dresser on the graveyard tour. "Listen to that hail."

"Not so fast, brother," said Gib. "Look at those walls and tell me what you see."

"Mosquito bills," said the tool dresser on the graveyard tour.

Then they all knew what was happening. The big mosquitoes were backing off and diving against the oil tank and ramming their bills right through it.

"Every man grab a hammer," yelled Gib, and picked up one himself and began bradding bills. Every time a mosquito bill came through, somebody was sure to clinch it.

This went on for an hour and a half until the walls of the tank were so thick with bradded mosquito bills that you couldn't put your hand on it without touching one. The critters on the outside were beating their wings and buzzing till they sounded like a hurricane in the Caribbean Sea. Presently they just naturally lifted that oil tank right up in the air and flew off with it.

⤚ MEDICINE WELLS

GIB KNEW THAT WITH MOSQUITOES
like that he could expect a lot of malaria, and that was the reason
he disobeyed orders. The next day he went out and geologized
around a while and made a location on an anticline that looked
promising. At three hundred feet he struck a vein of quinine.
Then he moved over five hundred feet to the northeast and at four
hundred feet brought in a five-barrel well of whisky. The crew
wanted to drill deeper and try to make a commercial producer out
of this well, but Gib said no. He had been sent to South America
to drill for oil. All he wanted was a little whisky for medicinal
purposes and five barrels would be enough. It was lucky they had
these wells, for down in that malaria country they couldn't have
brought in the big field they did if they hadn't had plenty of
medicine.

⤚ HOW GIB DISCOVERED STRICKIE

GIB HAD TROUBLE ENOUGH AS IT
was. If he had obeyed orders strictly he wouldn't have had any
trouble, but he wouldn't have brought in the field either. They
had told him to go down ten thousand feet unless he found oil
before he got that far and then to stop. So he had brought only
ten thousand feet of cable along. When he got to the end of the
cable, however, indications were mighty good and he wanted to go
a little further. His tool dresser said they would have to shut down
a month or two and wait for more rope to come from the States,
but Gib didn't like the idea. He hated to delay the work like that,
and then besides if the brass hats in New Jersey found out what he
was planning to do, they would more than likely stop him. It
wouldn't be the first time they had butted in and ruined a good
thing.

So Gib said he'd do a little figuring and look around a bit and
see what he could do. While Gib was thinking and studying he
started walking around, and pretty soon he was out in the jungle.
And as he walked along thinking and studying, he came upon a
big boa constrictor, a monstrous reptile, twenty blocks long if he
was one. The snake had just swallowed a lot of monkeys Gib
figured, for there was a monkey's tail sticking out of his mouth,
and he was lying there in a deep stupor not knowing Gib was
anywhere about.

Gib went back and got the crew and they dragged the snake back to the rig, spiked his head to a spoke in the bull wheel, wound him around the shaft, and spliced his tail to the cable. In a few minutes they were cutting ditch again. The snake made as good a drilling cable as you ever saw—a lot better than this new steel cable—with just enough give to make the tools handle easy. Everything went fine for an hour or two. Then the jarring woke the snake up and he began wiggling. The next thing Gib knew he had worked the spike loose and was running off with the whole string of tools. He made for the jungle and got away before Gib could stop him.

Gib hired a bunch of Indians to help him track the snake down. They trailed him for two weeks and finally found him five hundred miles from the rig. He had dragged the tools around so much that the drill stem was worn down to the size of a crowbar.

∽ HOW STRICKIE BAILED OUT

FORTUNATELY GIB HAD BROUGHT along another set of tools. He got to thinking about the way he had treated the big snake and he was downright ashamed of himself. He had found him sleeping peacefully and had dragged him off and driven a spike in his head and treated him rough. It was always better to be kind to dumb brutes.

So when Gib brought him back this time, he tried to win his friendship with kindness. First he went to the whisky well and got a barrel of whisky and gave it to him. When the snake had swallowed it, he began to wag his tail so friendly-like that Gib felt a deep affection for him. He named him Strickie, and every three weeks he fed him two hundred monkeys. He quit running at night so Strickie could have a rest, and each night when he shut down and unwound Strickie from the bull shaft, he gave him a barrel of whisky before he put him to bed. Strickie slept in front of Gib's bunkhouse door, and he wouldn't let man or beast come near until Gib ordered him down. It was not long until Strickie was the most valuable piece of equipment Gib had.

After Gib started drilling again and had let out about twenty feet of snake, he pulled the tools to bail out the cuttings. Then he realized how absent minded he had been. The sand line wasn't any longer than the drilling cable. If one wouldn't reach the bottom, the other wouldn't either. So the only thing he knew to do was to unwind Strickie and put him on the sand line. Gib was getting ready to tie his head to the line and his tail to the bucket, but Strickie kept changing ends on him. At first Gib thought he was just being playful. But from the way he kept wagging his tail and sticking it up against the end of the rope Gib saw that he wanted him to tie them together. Gib couldn't see that it made any difference, and so if Strickie preferred to go down head first, he was willing to let him.

As soon as Gib got the splice made, Strickie darted into the well and began to unwind the sand reel before Gib could stop him to tie on the bailer. He let him down to the bottom of the well and reeled him out. Strickie crawled to the sand pit and began to disgorge pumpings. From that time on Gib never used the bailer. Strickie had a bigger capacity and could clean the well with one lowering.

⌐ HOW GIB RECOVERED HIS TOOLS

AFTER GIB HAD BEEN USING STRICKIE about two weeks, the cable bootjacked off just above the rope socket. Gib let down a horn socket and caught the tools all right, but as he was trying to pull them out the latch in the socket broke and he lost them. And there he was with a string of tools in the well and no way to get them out.

He had his tool dresser fire up the forge and they went to work trying to make a new latch. While they were working, Strickie began wiggling so that he shook the whole rig. Gib realized that there wasn't any use in leaving him all wound up with the cable while they worked maybe the whole day on the horn socket. So he unwound him and gave him his whisky. As soon as he had swallowed it, Strickie crawled up on the derrick floor to the casing head and stuck his head in the well and began wagging his tail. Then Gib caught on to what was in his mind all along. He tied his tail to the cable and let him down. When he drew him up the tools came with him. Strickie had swallowed the rope socket, the sinker, the jars, and half the drill stem. Gib drilled a lot of wells after that and used a lot of newfangled equipment, but he never had a better fishing tool than Strickie.

↜ MORE CABLE

THE WELL WENT ALONG FINE. GIB hadn't found oil, but indications looked better and better every day. Gib's only worry was that Strickie might not be long enough to reach the oil he knew was down there. Each day there would be a little more of Strickie in the well and a little less on the bull wheels. When he shut down one Saturday night there was just enough of Strickie left to wrap once around the shaft. Gib had got a showing of oil that day, and he knew that he was right on top of something big and he stayed awake all night worrying about how to get to it.

But the next morning all his worries were over. That very night Strickie shed his skin and Gib had plenty of cable to finish the well.

↜ STRICKIE DELIVERS AGAIN

IT WAS A GUSHER, BUT GIB CLOSED it in and soon had it running into the storage. In no time at all it had filled the one thirty-thousand-barrel storage tank the mosquitoes had left. Gib shut it in and began laying a gathering line to the coast, where the big new tanker steamers that Standard had just put on could load. His pipe ran out when he was still about half a mile from the harbor, but by that time Strickie had shed again and his skin not only finished out the line but left enough over to reach up on deck and fill the compartments without all the bother of making pipe connections.

↜ STRICKIE'S LAST DAYS

GIB KEPT STRICKIE WITH HIM FOR years after that, and when Gib retired, Strickie retired too. The company gave him a pension and he lived in the Bronx, where he would have plenty of company. He still got his barrel of whisky every night and his two hundred monkeys every three weeks. Gib never came to New York without dropping by to see him.

⤳ THE SELF-DRILLING WELL

ONE DAY WHEN GIB WAS DRILLING in this South American field, he got to feeling kind of bad, like a fit of ague might be coming on. He told his tool dresser to watch her while he went down to the quinine and whisky wells and doctored himself up a bit. He took his medicine and lay down on his bunk to rest a few minutes, but he hadn't more than got stretched out when he heard the toolie yelling for him to come quick. When Gib asked him what was the matter he said he didn't know. He'd never seen a cable act like that before, and he didn't know what to do.

Gib took over, but he didn't know what to do either. The cable would throw slack and he'd give the temper screw a couple of turns upward, and then it would tighten up like a fiddle string. It whipped the sides of the well until it sounded like a hundred teamsters all cracking their whips at once as they used to back on Oil creek before the days of the pipe line; and before Gib had the trouble figured out, it snapped in two. He reeled out the cable, meaning to make up a string of fishing tools, but he soon discovered that the tools were still drilling. He could hear them strike the bottom, come up, go down and strike again. Then he noticed that the stroke was getting longer. Each time, the tools would come a little higher in the well. Pretty soon the rope socket was coming almost to the top.

The tool dresser hoisted the tongs and stood there ready to catch the stem when it came above the casing head, but Gib told him just to stand by and leave it alone until he told him to grab. It wasn't long before the rope socket was coming out of the well, then the sinker came, and then the jars. After the jars the drill stem and then the bit. Gib just stood there watching. The tools would go up into the derrick and when they came down, he would guide them back into the hole. It was clear now what had happened: he had struck a vein of rubber.

The tools went higher and higher. They knocked the crown block off the derrick. The toolie was itching to get the tongs on

79

them, but Gib said not yet. He just stood there watching the bit and guiding it back into the well. This went on for the rest of the day. By dusk the tools were going up so high that Gib had time to eat a sandwich between the going up and the coming down. Finally, once when the bit came up Gib noticed a piece of shale on it. He knew that the stratum of rubber had been penetrated.

"Now when she comes down, grab," he yelled.

The toolie caught the square shank of the sinker and held it with the tongs. They fixed up the broken crown block, attached the cable, and the next day they were drilling just as though nothing had happened. It wasn't many days until they brought in a good well.

PERPETUAL MOTION

GIB MOVED OVER A THOUSAND FEET to the north and put up the second rig, and here he lost his hole and a string of tools besides. It was the rubber formation again. Here the vein was thinner, and the tools never did get up enough momentum to come to the top. Gib and his tool dresser stood waiting with the tongs in hand for three days, but they discovered that the tools had reached their maximum height, and so they abandoned the hole. That was twenty odd years ago, but people who have been in the field recently say that the tools are still drilling—tons of steel going up and down, night and day, Sunday and week days—but the vein is not thick enough to throw the tools high enough to drill through it.

Gib had several other wells to drill in the region and he didn't want this to happen again. So he studied and studied and thought and invented his famous double-action, compensating jars. The mechanism of this device is rather complicated, but the principle is simplicity itself. A steel spring compensates for the elasticity of the rubber and enables the driller to go right on through a vein of rubber just as he would a stratum of shale or limestone or any other formation.

HOW GIB INVENTED RUBBER BOOTS

THIS WAS NOT GIB'S FIRST EXPERIENCE with rubber. Fact is that it was Gib that invented rubber boots, which in some respects was a mighty fine thing. But if he could have foreseen all the consequences of his invention, he never would have made it.

It all happened some twenty odd years ago when he was in East India putting down a bunch of wells for the Burmah Oil Company Limited.

When Gib went to the Fiji Islands he knew enough about the country to take along three or four extra pairs of boots for himself and each member of the crew. But it didn't occur to him to do this when he went to India. He had always heard that India was the seat of an ancient and mature civilization, and he naturally assumed that in a civilized country one would be able to buy shoes wherever he went. When he got there, however, he noticed that all the natives who didn't wear sandals were barefooted; and when his boots began to wear out, he started looking for a new pair. He went to every store for a hundred miles around, but not one pair of boots or shoes of any kind could he find for sale. He and his men patched up their boots the best they could. They cut off pieces of belting for soles, but the uppers were getting more and more ragged and they saw that it wouldn't be long until they would be barefooted like the natives. The men were getting madder and madder and were threatening to quit and go back to God's country where a man could buy a pair of Wisconsin boots if he had the money.

Gib saw that something had to be done if the work was to go on, so he studied and studied and after a while he hit upon a solution so simple that he wondered why he had not thought of it before—especially since he was right in the middle of the rubber country where the natives were bringing in gum from the forests every day.

First he got some pure para gum. Then he took off his boots, that is as much of his boots as was left, which was just barely enough to hang to his feet, and covered his socks with a layer of rubber, making the soles especially thick. When he got them done he had the other men take off their boots, that is what was left of them, and he covered their socks in the same way.

In some ways the new boots were better than leather, especially when the rainy season came. The men were pleased and went about their work with a new will and cut more ditch per day than they had ever done before.

Then just as everybody was feeling happy a most unfortunate accident occurred. One day Gib's tool dresser climbed the derrick to grease the crown pulleys. Gib never did know how it came

81

about, for he was a good workman and had never done anything like that before, but for some reason he fell off. He hit the ground rubber boots first and bounced up twice as high as the derrick. When he hit the ground the second time, he bounced out of sight and didn't come down for two hours. When he went up the third time, he didn't come down for two days. Gib got to figuring, and he figured it out that if he went up again, he wouldn't come down in less than twenty-four days, and Gib knew that no man could live for twenty-four days without food or drink. So as much as he hated to do it, Gib had to shoot him to keep him from starving to death.

↰ HOW GIB SAVED HIS TOOL DRESSER

IF, HOWEVER, GIB HAD THEN KNOWN some of the things he later learned when he was drilling in the big pasture country of West Texas he could have saved the poor toolie's life and himself all the regret he felt every time he got to thinking about having invented rubber boots.

Fact is he was so cut up about the tool dresser that when he got back to the United States, he didn't feel like taking out a patent on his invention. If he had he would have been a rich man, for it wasn't long before rubber boots began to appear in all the oil fields of the United States. Gib remembered the first pair ever seen in the Bradford area. He was drilling there at the time, and one midnight his tool dresser came on tour with a pair on. It was raining and the ground was muddy all around the rig. About two o'clock in the morning it began to freeze, and by daylight the derrick was a cone of ice and the ground was as hard as pavement. The crown pulley got to squeaking and the toolie said he would go up and grease it. Gib told him to be careful and he said he would. He greased the pulley all right but on his way down he slipped and fell. He began bouncing just as the toolie in India had done and was soon out of sight.

Gib cut the bailer loose, tied a hondo in the sand line, and made a loop just as he had seen the cowboys do in Texas. When the tool dresser came down and started up again, Gib lassoed him around the neck, threw in the clutch and reeled him in. The man was forever grateful to him for saving him from a horrible death.

IN ALL HIS YEARS OF DRILLING GIB
never had a law suit. But he came mighty near it one time. He
was working for a company in Ohio. It wasn't a very big propo-
sition, and as it turned out he was glad that it wasn't. Most of the
acreage was leased before his company got in there, and all they
could get was a hundred-and-sixty-acre farm, a wedge-shaped piece
of land in Washington county, at least two miles from production.

At the depth of a thousand feet Gib struck a vein of granite that
would take the edge off of a bit in no time at all. He spent more
time pulling tools and dressing bits than he did in drilling. Even
then he couldn't keep a flare on the bit. It would stick in the hole;
he would jar it loose and dress it, and it would stick again. This
went on from twelve to four o'clock in the afternoon, when the
tools lodged so tight he couldn't budge them an inch. He knew
that he was in for a fishing job that was a real fishing job.

He ran a knife down the sand line and cut the cable a few feet
above the rope socket. Then he rigged up the longest string of
fishing tools ever let down in an oil well. On the bottom was a
rope spear to catch the cable end. Above that was a sinker, and
above that a pair of long-stroke fishing jars, then a sinker and
another pair of jars. He put on so many sinkers and jars that he
couldn't keep count of them and had to send for a bookkeeper.
Then came the drill stem and rope socket.

Gib lowered the string into the well and right away he caught
the tools. Then began the job of jarring them loose. He worked
all the rest of the afternoon, but when dark came he couldn't tell
that he'd moved them an inch. At ten o'clock that night they were
still as tight as ever. At midnight they were still stuck, but Gib and
his toolie were glad to see twelve o'clock come so they could go
home and sleep and let the other tour do the fishing for a while.
But the other tour didn't come. At twelve-thirty they still hadn't
showed up. The tool dresser wanted to quit and go to bed, but Gib
told him they'd better work on a while longer. He'd see that the
other men made it up to them some time.

They worked until two o'clock and still no relief came. Gib told
the toolie to watch her a while and he would walk back to the
boarding house and see what was the matter. Gib hadn't gone far
when he found himself on the edge of a precipice. It was pretty

dark that night and he was lucky that he didn't walk right off of it. Down below he saw a lantern and heard hammering and sawing.

"What are you doing down there?" he yelled.

"Hello, Gib," the other driller answered. "We're building a ladder. We're trying to get up to the well."

Gib had jarred the whole lease up seventy-five feet. The graveyard tour had come out at twelve as they were supposed to, and had found the precipice and had begun work on the ladder right away. But as Gib kept jarring the lease higher, they had to go back several times for more lumber, and even then the lease was gaining on them.

A SIMPLE SOLUTION

GIB SHUT DOWN AND THEY FINISHED the ladder. It was daylight and they were still wondering what to do when the farmer who owned the land came out and said he was going to have the law on him for ruining his farm. He had gathered a load of corn the day before and was ready to take it to market and his wife was going with him, and they had got up before daylight to get an early start, and there they were stuck up seventy-five feet in the air and no way to get down, and the farm would never be worth anything again. Now Gib knew that the lease had a clause in it about damage to crops and premises, and he was afraid that the company was in for a lawsuit. However, he gave the man a drink out of a jug he kept around the rig for emergencies and told him that if he would give him a little time, he thought he could fix it up.

So Gib began thinking and studying and before long he hit upon a solution so simple that he wondered why he hadn't thought of it sooner. He sent to a big medicine house and got forty barrels of arnica salve, hoisted them up to the rig on the sand line, and packed the salve into the well. In an hour and a half the lease had fallen two feet. By the end of the second day the swelling was completely gone and the rock was so softened that the tools came out with no more trouble than bealing out a splinter.

⤳ GIB'S NARROWEST ESCAPE

GIB HAD HAD MANY A NARROW escape in his day, what with bears in Russia, mosquitoes in New Jersey, and cannibals in the Fiji Islands. But the narrowest escape he ever had was in the calm and peaceful English countryside.

The syndicate that Gib had worked for in the Fiji Islands decided to do a little exploring around home, and they sent Gib to put up a rig and put down a well. He had considerable trouble getting the derrick up on account of the fog. It was so thick that they couldn't see from one girt to another. But they did the best they could and finally one day by noon there was nothing left to do but to shingle the roof on the band-wheel house, a job that they thought they could finish in an hour or so. But at four o'clock in the afternoon they were still nailing on shingles, and at six they were still working.

Then the sun came out for just a moment, and roof and men came down with a crash. They had passed the eaves long ago and had been shingling the fog.

⤳ GIB AS MANUFACTURER

ALTHOUGH GIB MORGAN'S CHIEF mission in life was to drill oil wells, he did from time to time engage in other activities, sometimes from choice and sometimes from necessity.

Back in '73 it was necessity. That was the year when the first big shutdown came. The producers in the oil region of Pennsylvania shut down all their old wells and stopped drilling new ones in an effort to make John D. pay them more for their crude. Gib, like all the other drillers in the field, found himself without a job. That was a panic year too, and jobs in other places were as scarce as they were in the oil region.

Gib didn't like the idea of sitting around doing nothing, so he began thinking and studying, and after a little he hit upon an idea by which he thought he could turn an honest penny and create employment too. He went up the Clarion River and for less than a song he bought the timber rights on some old cut-over land upon which there wasn't a thing but stumps. Then he went through the oil country and hired a gang of unemployed tool dressers and put them to work making shoe pegs. They would saw the stumps into cross sections the length of the pegs, split them into the proper sizes, and sharpen one end.

They worked all winter and when spring came they had made so many pegs that Gib had to charter two big barges to take them to market. He floated them to Pittsburgh, then down the Ohio and Mississippi to St. Louis, where the big shoe factories were located. But when he got to St. Louis, the shoemakers had all gone on strike, and he couldn't sell so much as one bushel of pegs.

It looked as though Gib was going to lose all his investment, which was all the capital he had. He studied a while, and then he had an idea. He got his men together and had them sharpen the other ends of the pegs. Then he took them to a big grain dealer and sold them for oats. He didn't get rich, but he made enough to tide him over until drilling started again.

↜ GIB AS FARMER

GIB'S VENTURES INTO AGRICULTURE were less successful, but since his planting was done in spare time for recreation, his failures were of little consequence.

Once he decided to make a home garden. He thought it would be an economy of land and labor to plant his corn and beans together so that the bean vines could run on the corn stalks. Somehow the timing went wrong. The corn grew faster than the beans and pulled the vines up by the roots.

Then once when he was living in Texas, he put in a big field of pop corn. It was a good crop that year, and he harvested all the pop corn he could pack into his barn. Then along in late summer came the hottest day in forty years. Gib was lying in the shade of a hackberry tree trying to keep cool when he heard a series of explosions that sounded like musketry in battle. He looked up in time to see the roof blown off the barn and the pop corn spouting up like a twenty-thousand-barrel gusher, only white.

As the popped grains fell to the earth, Gib's old gray mule thought they were snowflakes and froze to death.

CUCUMBERS IN INDIA

STRANGE AS IT MAY SEEM, ONE OF Gib's agricultural failures was caused by too much success, or maybe he should say that the soil was too fertile.

It was while Gib was drilling in India, and a great drouth hit the country. All vegetation dried up. The animals all got so poor they couldn't stand up without leaning against each other.

Then the rains came and in a few days grass was belly high to an elephant. Then Gib remembered that he had a package of cucumbers seeds that his congressman from Pennsylvania had mailed to him. He thought he might as well plant them, although he really didn't expect to be there when they bore. He cleared off a plot of ground, fenced it with a strong rail fence, and spaded it up. He prepared a fine seed bed and then starting planting. He got down on his knees and pressed the seeds into the soil with his thumb.

When he got about half way across the pen on his first row, he felt something crawling up his leg. He looked around expecting to see some sort of reptile or giant tropical insect. What he saw was a cucumber vine. The seeds had come up and the vines were threatening to entangle him. Gib fled for his life. He managed to get to the fence, but the vines had enwrapped him so that he couldn't get over it, and while he was struggling they were binding him faster and faster to the fence.

Then it occurred to him that his only hope was to cut himself loose. He reached into his pocket for his jack knife and pulled out a ten-inch cucumber.

GIB AS DAIRYMAN

AT ONE TIME GIB OWNED THE biggest dairy in the state of New York. He hadn't planned to go into the business; he just drifted into it more or less by accident. He was working in the oil field at Olean when the town was booming and there was a milk shortage. When it got to where Gib couldn't get cream for his coffee, he bought a cow of his own.

She looked like a good cow, and for a while she gave more milk than he needed and he sold the surplus. Then she began giving a little bit less each day. He bought her expensive foods that were supposed to bring her yield up, but they didn't do any good. He called in a veterinarian, who charged him a big fat fee, but didn't get him any more milk. He talked to the experts at Cornell, and they gave him free advice, but as they advised him more and more, the cow gave less and less. She was down to two ounces a day, and Gib knew she wouldn't hold up to that figure much longer.

He thought and studied, and then it occurred to him that he might try a treatment he had seen applied successfully to oil wells that had got sluggish from the formations of coatings of paraffin or asphalt on the walls of the hole. He measured the cow, multiplied her length by her diameter in inches and divided by 72, the result being 20.

He shot her with twenty quarts of nitroglycerin. He never had to milk her again. From that time on she flowed at the rate of ten gallons a day.

The success of this experiment prompted Gib to go in for dairying on a large scale. He went through the dairy region buying up for practically nothing all the cows that were failing, and shot them back into production, usually at a higher yield than ever. He produced so much milk that the express trains couldn't carry it to the city, and he had to put in his own pipe line.

꒰   GIB'S BOARDING HOUSE

When he was in West Virginia, Gib Morgan, more as an accommodation to his friends than anything else, put up a boarding house for oil field workers. The thing that made his place famous was his buckwheat pancakes. The men would crowd his place every morning and demand more and more hot cakes. Gib had to enlarge his dining room and get more and larger griddles. But he still couldn't keep ahead of his trade.

So he finally had to build a new plant altogether. He bought a dozen of the largest concrete mixers he could find and steam engines to turn them and set them on a hill a mile away. Into these mixers his workmen dumped flour and milk and eggs and other ingredients—the exact recipe is still a trade secret—and when the batter had reached a certain creamy consistency it was turned into a pipe line leading to the kitchen. The griddles were bottoms of 43,000-barrel oil tanks, each heated by a gas well underneath it. At first Gib had trouble keeping the irons greased, but he solved that problem by strapping sides of fat bacon to the feet of strong Negroes and having them skate over the irons. Seven big strapping men skimmed over the hot surface of each griddle continuously. They were followed by another crew who handled the batter hoses leading from the pipe line. Another crew with shovels turned the cakes over, and a fourth took them up and tossed them to the waiters.

Melted butter and maple syrup flowed through pipes along the half-mile counters, and at each seat were spigots from which the customer drew as much as he wanted.

Gib fed twenty-five thousand oil field workers at a time. So many people came out of mere curiosity to see Gib's place that they were about to crowd out his regular customers, so Gib had to put up a sign: ONLY DRILLERS AND TOOL DRESSERS FED HERE.

↳ GIB'S HOTEL

BUT AFTER SPINDLETOP CAME IN and Gib came to Texas and saw the thousands of people that were crowding Beaumont without any place to stay, he decided he would put up a hotel for the general public. The building was forty stories high with ten high-speed elevators to bring the people up and down. When they stepped out of the elevator, no matter which floor, there was a narrow gauge railroad with a train waiting to take them to their rooms. In each room was a number of taps— one for ice water, one for Bourbon, one for rye, and one for Scotch, one for Tom Collins, one for old fashioned, and so on.

But the most remarkable thing about the hotel was its adaptation to the climate. Gib had noticed that throughout Texas and Oklahoma when a guest came in, he always asked for a south or east room. He never wanted a north or west room. So Gib built his hotel without any north or west rooms. Every guest who registered would be assigned to a south or east room. This would go on until all the rooms were filled. Every guest would go to bed in a room with a south or east exposure. But when those who had gone to bed first would wake up in the morning, they would look out through north or west windows and see the railroad tracks.

Gib's hotel was mounted on a turntable, but by the time his guests found it out, they were so pleased with the service, especially the spigot service, that they didn't mind.

↶ TROUBLE WITH THE CROWN PULLEY

ONE TIME BACK IN 1872 GIB WAS drilling over here in Butler county, Pennsylvania. He had an old second-hand engine that gave him a lot of trouble from the start. One day it would blow a cylinder head, and he'd patch it up, and it would run a day or two and then something else would happen. When he was down about two hundred feet, it just naturally played out entirely and he had to send it to the machine shop in Eau Claire to have it overhauled. The roads were belly deep in mud and teaming was slow. It was two weeks before he got it back.

When it came he set it up and got up steam. He was about ready to lower the tools when he remembered that they hadn't greased the crown pulley. He sent the tool dresser up to do it. The toolie got it greased all right, and then he gave a yell loud enough to wake up the dead and started coming down that ladder a whole lot faster than he had gone up. While they were shut down the hornets had built a nest under the crown block and one had stung the toolie on the arm.

Gib knew what to do for a sting. He ran out into the woods and got leaves from seven kinds of trees, bruised them and made a poultice and bound it to the tool dresser's arm. Gib told him to sit on the lazy bench for a while and he would go ahead and lower the tools and start drilling.

The tools moved about a foot and wouldn't go any further. Gib couldn't find anything wrong on the ground. Something seemed to be keeping the cable from going through the pulley. Gib climbed the derrick. He found a knot on the cable as big as a Georgia watermelon.

He climbed down and took the poultices off the toolie's arm, went back up the derrick and wrapped it around the cable. He hated to do the poor toolie that way, but he had to do something. In a half hour the swelling was gone and drilling was under way.

↶ GIB MORGAN'S WONDERFUL HORSE

ONE TIME WHEN GIB MORGAN was drilling in Kentucky, a farm hand came by one day leading a wobbly colt. He stopped to look at the rig and Gib got to talking to him and asked him what he was doing to do with the colt. He said he was taking him out to the woods to knock him in the head because the Colonel didn't know who his daddy was. He said he didn't want to do it, but orders were orders. Gib didn't know whether the fellow was playing him for a sucker or not, but he sort of took a fancy to the colt and said he'd give him ten dollars for it.

"I'm taking a big risk," the farm hand said, "but if you'll be sure you don't let the Colonel know, you can have him."

Gib raised the colt by hand. He named him Torpedo, for the Roberts torpedo used to shoot oil wells. Torpedo turned out to be a fine animal. Fact is Gib didn't know how he ever could have managed to get along without Torpedo—especially after he got to be production superintendent for Standard Oil of New Jersey. He never would have got around to all the places he had to go if he had had to go on the trains.

For example one morning he was in Oil City, Pennsylvania, when it was time for one of his drillers to bring in a well at Coffeyville, Kansas, that afternoon. He saddled Torpedo about nine o'clock in the morning and started out. He rode by the Louisiana field to inspect some wells in progress there, oversaw the drilling in and the capping of the well in Kansas, and got back to Oil City for late supper.

If you don't believe Gib could have done that, you haven't seen Torpedo. He was no ordinary horse. He weighed twenty tons and was twenty-two yards long if he was one.

Turn him around? He didn't turn him around. He just threw him in reverse.

⌐ TORPEDO'S CHARIOT RACE

WHEN THEY SENT GIB TO ITALY to do some wildcat drilling there, he took his horse with him. He set up several rigs and when they seemed to be coming along all right, Gib got on Torpedo one day and cantered over to Rome to see the sights. There was a lot of excitement about a big chariot race that was to take place in the Coloseum in about a week, with sweepstakes amounting to fifty thousand dollars. Gib entered Torpedo, but he was careful not to let the people in charge see him.

The next thing was to find a chariot. There wasn't any in all Rome big enough for his horse. He went back to the lease and studied a while and got to looking at the rig, and pretty soon he had an idea. He screwed some lengths of casing together for shafts and took a pair of bull wheels and made one of the neatest chariots you ever saw.

Great cheers greeted him as he drove into the Coloseum. Torpedo was always a little slow in getting started, but in three seconds he took the lead. As Gib passed the other chariots it looked like they were standing still. The next thing he knew the bull wheels were on fire. But he gave Torpedo the reins and finished up on the axle, at least ten lengths ahead of his nearest competitor.

ᔐ TORPEDO IN DANGER

TORPEDO LIVED TO A RIPE OLD AGE, but Gib almost lost him once while he was still in his prime. Gib had ridden him over to New Jersey to confer with John D. and other High Powers of Standard Oil, and he couldn't find any stable in town big enough to put him up in. So the only thing to do was to ride out into the country and camp. He staked Torpedo out, unrolled his bedding, lay down, and was just dozing off, when he heard such a pitiful whinny that it made his heart bleed. He looked up just in time to see a bunch of mosquitoes pick poor Torpedo up by the back and shake his shoes off. Gib fired into them with his twenty-four-barrel shotgun. He brought down ten. The other six dropped Torpedo and fled before he could reload.

ᔐ GIB MORGAN'S CONTRIBUTION TO GEOLOGY

DURING THE EARLY DAYS OF THE oil industry there was a lot of discussion about the nature of oil deposits. One school of learned men said they were reservoirs; another school of equally learned men held they were veins. All of which shows that nobody else knows as much about oil as the practical oil man. For Gib Morgan demonstrated beyond a shadow of a doubt that all the learned men were wrong. Oil deposits are running streams, something like creeks and rivers, but not quite like them either, for the water in a river can never run up hill. They are more like big pipe lines that can dip up and down and the oil will dip up and down too, going as high as its source. If you find oil more often in anticlines than synclines, the reason is very simple: the oil is closer to the surface there.

Gib made this discovery quite by accident. It began back in the seventies when he was working in the Bradford field. He had just drilled into the oil sand and was measuring the depth of the well. That was before Van Ostand invented his automatic measuring device. Gib worked it by tying strings on the sand line. He had the bailer on the bottom of the well and was bent over tying a string at the top of the casing, when his watch slipped out of his pocket and fell into the well.

It was a good watch—gold case and twenty-one jeweled works—and he hated to lose it. He tried for a couple of hours to bail it out, but he didn't have any luck. He couldn't get it out, and he wanted to drill about twenty feet into the oil sand, and so there was nothing to do but go ahead and drill it to pieces. When he bailed out he examined the cuttings carefully, but didn't find so much as the hairspring. Where that watch went was a mystery to him for a long time.

Fourteen years later he was drilling in West Virginia. One time when he emptied the sand bucket, he saw something shining in the slush pit. He fished it out and there was the watch he had dropped in the well at Bradford. There couldn't be any kind of doubt. Gib would have known that watch anywhere.

But what was more remarkable it was still running. And when he compared it with the watch in his pocket, they were exactly together. The watch hadn't lost a second in all those fourteen years in the bowels of the earth.

No, it hadn't run down. It was a stem winder and as the current of oil had carried it along, the stem had scraped on the bottom and sides of the passage and this had kept it wound up.

Gib still had the watch among his things at home and would show it to anybody who wanted to see it.

⌐ GIB AS DOCTOR

ONE REASON WHY GIB ALWAYS felt secure was that he knew if the oil played out, he could find some other way of making a living. For example he could go into

93

the patent medicine business. He had a discovery of his own that he could put on the market if he ever had to.

One time Gib's health began to fail him. He didn't hurt anywhere in particular and he wasn't sick enough to go to bed. Didn't even quit work, as a matter of fact. He just got weaker and weaker every day. What made it harder to understand was that he had a good appetite and ate three big meals every day. But they didn't seem to do him any good. He just got hungrier and weaker and tireder every day.

He went to several doctors and they gave him tonics and bitters and liver pills, but he kept getting no better fast, and he decided he'd better do something for himself. So he thought and studied and read up, and he finally came to the conclusion that he had a tape worm.

The next question was how to get rid of it. He bought several bottles of different kinds of medicines that were supposed to remove tape worms, but after he took them he still had his tape worm. So he had to make his own medicine. Just what it contained was a trade secret that Gib might use some day if he ever went broke. He would say, however, that one of the ingredients was Epsom salts.

On the day Gib took the first dose of the medicine, he went to work as usual. The salts acted sooner than he expected it to, and the only place he could find to hide was back of a thirty-eight-thousand barrel oil tank. He passed three feet of tape worm, including the head, but he knew that wasn't all. He tied the worm's head to a pipe connection and began running around the tank. After he had circled it forty times, friction had generated enough heat to burn the worm in two, and he never did know how long it was.

⤴ GIB'S GUNS

GIB MORGAN WAS ONE OF THE busiest men in the world. If he hadn't been, he couldn't have done all the things he did—not in one man's lifetime. Yet he did manage to find time for a little recreation now and then, generally fishing or hunting.

His fame as a hunter depended in some part upon two very remarkable and famous guns he owned, both of which he had designed himself and had had manufactured at no inconsiderable cost. One was a fine rifle with a telescope sight, the first ever placed on a gun. He used to hunt wild pigs with it—javelinas they called them in Texas. He could climb a mesa or even a slight hill, and survey the country for thirty miles around. If there was a drove of javelinas anywhere within that radius, he could focus his telescope sight on them and draw them up to where he could hear them grunt. The rest was easy. All he had to do was pull the trigger. He couldn't miss them. But shooting at such long range, he found that the meat would often spoil before he could get to it. He thought and studied a while and then it occurred to him to salt his bullets. After that he had no trouble.

Equally famous was his fowling piece, a twenty-four-barrel shotgun. He designed it for shooting the passenger pigeons that used to fly over Clarion valley in such numbers that they blotted out the sun. When a flock passed over, even if it was twelve o'clock sun time, the cows came home to be milked and the chickens went to roost.

Gib never would forget the first time he shot his gun. It had just come from the gunsmith's a few days before, and Gib had been waiting for the pigeons. One day they came. He got out his new fowling piece, loaded all twenty-four barrels to the muzzle, and rushed to the woods. By that time it was too dark for him to see more than ten feet in front of him. He raised the gun to his shoulder, pointed it toward the sky and fired all twenty-four barrels. That was the last he knew for some time. When he came to, he thought his folks must have picked him up for dead and buried him alive. He began struggling, however, more from instinct than conviction, and after an hour or so he saw sunlight.

He had been knocked through the top soil and three feet into the hardpan and buried in pigeons seventy-two feet deep.

That surely was a lesson to him. After that he loaded his gun only half way to the muzzle.

GIB'S DOGS

GIB HAD OWNED A LOT OF GOOD hunting dogs in his day, three of them very famous. One was a little white fice, the best rabbit dog in the whole state of Pennsylvania. He could worm his way into the underbrush, and if there were a rabbit anywhere in it he could find it and chase it out. And he was fast too. It wasn't often that a rabbit got away from him.

95

One day this little fice routed a rabbit and began chasing it down the hill so fast that rabbit and dog looked like one grey streak. The rabbit, seeing that it could not outrun the dog, stopped suddenly and the dog ran over him and crashed headlong into the stump of a sapling which had been broken off in a storm and from which a sharp splinter projected. The splinter split the dog in two from the tip of his nose to the tip of his tail. Gib was terribly put out when he saw his little white fice lying there in two pieces. But he did not take time to grieve. He grabbed up the halves, rubbed them with Kier's Senneca oil, a bottle of which he always carried in his pocket for such emergencies, slapped them together and put them down. The dog ran on after the rabbit and soon caught it. Gib thought there was something queer about the way the dog ran, but he went so fast that he couldn't be sure what it was. As the fice brought the rabbit up to Gib, he discovered that he had been a bit hasty in putting him together. He had put two legs up and two legs down. It turned out, however, that he had unwittingly made an improvement on nature. The dog could run faster than ever. He simply spun around like a cartwheel with such momentum that he could overhaul any rabbit in the Allegheny valley. He was the fastest and most famous rabbit dog in Pennsylvania.

Gib neglected to take out a patent, however, and it wasn't long before his neighbors began splitting their dogs open and putting them back together in imitation of Gib's.

Gib also had a coon dog that might have become as famous as the fice had he not come to an untimely end. One day when Gib was cutting logs for a hut near a wildcat location, he heard the hound baying. He went to the dog and found that he had dug out a ground hog and was trying to catch it. He wasn't having any luck, however, for when the dog would leap into the hole, the ground hog would leap out; and when the dog would leap out, the ground hog would leap in. This went on for a long time, until the dog got so hot and tired that Gib got sorry for him, and he thought he'd better just kill the ground hog himself. As it leaped from the hole, Gib struck at it with the axe. But the dog was quicker than he realized. It was the dog's head he cut off.

Gib was awfully blue about killing his faithful coon dog, but he had one comfort: it happened so quick that he was convinced to this day that the dog never knew for sure whether it was Gib or the ground hog that killed him.

96

Of course this reversible fice, fast though he was, could not keep pace with Gib's wolf dog, a greyhound, the only pet Gib ever had that could keep up with Torpedo. For years he was Gib's constant companion wherever he went.

Gib never would forget the time he took him to St. Louis. When he was about to get on the train—the fastest on the Pennsylvania line—the conductor stopped him. He said he didn't allow dogs in the coaches, but Gib could put him in the baggage car. Gib said he'd just lead him. So he tied him to the rear coach, giving him about twenty feet of leash.

In about an hour the conductor came around and told Gib that the train was going a hundred and fifty miles an hour and that he had better see about his dog. Gib went back but couldn't see the dog anywhere. He climbed down on the steps and looked under the coach. There was his hound running along on three legs.

He hadn't been crippled. One of the wheels had developed a hot box and the dog was trying to cool it off.

∽ GIB IN RUSSIA

GIB REGRETTED THAT HE DID NOT take his firearms with him when he went to Russia to put down some wells in the Baku area. They would have saved him a lot of agony, although as it turned out, he really didn't need them.

He had heard a lot about Russian bears all his life, and he used to see a few occasionally hanging around the outskirts of the oil camps, but it did not occur him to him that they were really dangerous.

Then one day in the fall of the year the snow storms came. The snow fell steadily for a week and still showed no signs of letting up. By that time grub was getting low at the camp and it was clear that somebody had to go to town and get some groceries. Now Gib never called on his men to do anything he wouldn't do himself. He told a couple of toolies to hitch up the two little Russian ponies they had to the sleigh and he'd drive to a town about twenty miles away and bring home some food.

Gib put on his fur overcoat and cap, wrapped himself in heavy robes and started out through the blinding snow. He had not gone more than half way when the horses began pricking up their ears and snorting. He looked back, and through the falling snow he made out the forms of two of the biggest bears he had ever seen. They were running neck and neck, following the track of the sleigh, and gaining on it every minute. Gib whipped the horses, but without increasing their speed. From sheer fear of the bears they were already running as fast as they could.

The bears were now within three feet of the sleigh. Gib quit whipping the horses and began whipping the bears, but they paid no attention to him. Then he saw them pause and gather their legs for a leap. He crouched under the robes and covered his head. He waited for what seemed to him hours and nothing happened. The sleigh moved on, it seemed to him, a little faster than before. He peeked out from under the robes. The bears were drawing the sleigh. They had leaped over him and eaten the horses right into the harness and Russian yoke.

Gib picked up the lines, drove them into town, loaded the sleigh with grub, and drove back to camp. By that time the bears were as gentle as ponies. He drove them all winter.

GIB AS FISHERMAN

All his life Gib had heard of the big catfish in the lower Mississippi river. So one time when he was down in Louisiana looking after the oil wells of his company, he decided to take a day off and go fishing. He didn't want to be bothered with little fish that ordinary tackle would hold, so he fixed up an outfit for the great-granddaddies. He cut a big southern pine for a pole. He got a spool of drilling cable for a line and a steamboat anchor for a hook. He baited the hook with a young steer, and threw out into the deep water.

He waited a while, but nothing happened. But he wasn't discouraged. He knew the big fellows were slow to bite and that there wasn't anything to do but to give them time. He stuck the butt of the pole into the mud and sat down on it. Pretty soon he dozed off to sleep.

Suddenly he found himself being dragged toward the river. He jumped up and pulled with all his might and tossed a big catfish clear over his head. When it landed in the brush it sounded like a big hemlock falling, and the way it thrashed around in the brush you would have thought a hurricane had struck the cane break.

Gib never did know how big the monster was, for he was afraid to get close enough to it to find out. But he did notice that when that cat came out of the river, the water level fell two feet.

⤴ GIB MORGAN'S FIGHT

GIB MORGAN WAS A PEACEFUL AND law-abiding man whose motto was Live and Let Live. He tried to get along with everybody, and he generally did. In fact during his long career as a tool dresser, driller, pipe liner, production superintendent and what not, he had only one fight and he wouldn't have had it if he could have helped it.

Gib was working for a pipe line company bossing a gang of nigger ditch diggers along the Ohio river. They were all fine hands but one. This one was a big buck who thought he knew more than Gib. He wouldn't do his work right, and when Gib would jack him up, he would give him a lot of back talk. Gib saw that he would have to curb him a little bit or he would ruin the whole gang. So one day when he was particularly sassy, Gib corrected him with a pair of forty-eight-inch pipe tongs.

Well, that nigger grabbed Gib around the waist and they both rolled into the Ohio river and sank to the bottom. The next thing Gib knew the nigger had drawn a knife and started to whittle on him. Gib had to protect himself. He drew out his jack knife and started to work on the nigger. Then began the most God-awful battle that ever took place in the United States.

All the men on the gang stopped work and lined up along the river bank to watch the fight. The news spread and more people came. The railroads ran excursion trains to the scene, and all the steamboats stopped and tied up. The farmers on both sides of the river charged for standing room and cleared over fifty thousand dollars. Tens of thousands of dollars were bet on the outcome of the fight.

The only way the spectators had of knowing how the battle was going was by watching for the pieces of flesh that came to the surface of the water. When there were more pieces of white-skinned flesh than black-skinned flesh coming up, the odds were in favor of the nigger. When there were more pieces of black-skinned than white-skinned flesh coming up, the odds were in favor of Gib. Not all the pieces, however, came up. When the catfish found out what was going on, they gathered from miles up and down the river for a big feast. Every once in a while one would swim between Gib and the nigger and get cut to pieces.

No, Gib didn't kill the nigger.

They fought and they fought until finally their knives got so dull they wouldn't cut any more. They agreed to a truce so they could come up and grind their blades. When they came out they discovered they had been fighting for two weeks, and they were powerfully hungry. They went to a restaurant and each ordered a beefsteak four inches thick. When they had finished eating, they felt so good they called the fight off.

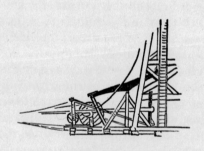

APPENDIX

Gib Morgan's Contributions to S. W. Munn's

Useful Information for Oil Men

A LETTER FROM OUR OLD FRIEND, GIB. MORGAN

National Military Home,
Grant Co., Indiana,
March 17, 1900.

Mr. S. W. Munn,

Mannington, W. Va.

Dear Old Friend.—In reply to youre letter of recent date, I will say the soldiers home is a wourld within its self, all walks of life are here represented, But you may not be awair that we have inventiv genises of more than ordinary calibra although history refuses to record the benefits to mankind resulting from any of our inventive labors.

I will now give you the modis oprinda of one of my mechanical wonders. There were not long since in our town a superabundance of cats, which by their hidious youling and nocturnal prowling made refreshing sleep dificut or imposible, the good people of the town naturly turned their faces toward me to devise some means whereby to rid them selves of the disturbing element of their rest. I therefore betook my self to my labitory for silent undisturbed study, and within the perid of time it takes a methidist preacher to write his sunday sermon I made a machine concisting of wire nails knives circler saws and springs so arainged as to emit youling and screaching growling and scratching nois duplicating a cat, then I wound her up and set her, All the felines in town would assemble to investigate they would hoult in front of my machine with backs elevated fured tails arect and with dialated eyes viewing a veritable cat confined in an iner room visible to themselves until their pugnosios naturs could not indure it no longer, Then the boldest would spring vishousls [sic] as he suposed toward his chalanger, (but he never came back) he was toren and ridled into sreds by my machine, others becoming bolder by their companions patriotic example would fly at the imaginary cat and only to meet the same fragrementery destiny. I have aplyed for a patent on my invincible double acting Cat exterminator.

101

SOME STORIES BY GIB MORGAN

I was Emploed by the (The hard able and scarcely ever get Oil Co,) Capitalized at $5,000,000,000.00. with paid in capital of $300.00. with head quarters at Pittsburg, Pa.

To go down in west verginia and lease evry thing in sight, My salry was to be $100.00, per month with eating drinking and washing, Well the first day I got as far as Wheeling, W, Va, Say boys was you ever in Wheeling? Ge Whiz: they keep some mighty fine liquor there, McDonald is not in it, well after vesiting some of the officials of the town I went out about sixty miles in the interior, and talking about steep hills and mountains you could not find level ground enough to grease a wagon on had to chain it to a stump Reach out of the third story window and lock the sellar door, Look up the chimley and cee the cows coming home, there was a man fel out of a cornfield in to the river we cot him with a horn socket after runing out about fifteen hundred feet of cable, I was riding a mule near Glovers Gap when I met a man with leaky chin whiskers and a gun I said that I was afraid to ride the mule down the mountain as it was to steep and I would just lead him down, Oh no he said just sit on his back, the animals in this country are all sure footed, well I started and when I got about half ways down the mountain I felt some thing warm on the back of my neck I just run my hand under my overcoat collar and raked out about a half peck of mule dung, you will observe that the mountains are almost purpindicler.

One eavning I as setting on the poarch of a native and his wife, I noticed a drove of hogs near by, I asked the lady if they raised many porkers in that country, After taking something out of a little tin box she said there was about twenty nine thousand in that drove the ballance of them was out on the hills, There wer big hogs little hogs and spoted hogs, I noticed one pecluarity about these hogs they all had a round hole in the right ear, I asked the man if they all belonged to the same party I suposed the hole to be a mark, Oh no not by any means he said that they wer all born that way they would clime the mountain in search of acorns and when the wanted to come down they would just thrust their hind leg through the hole and ruflock them selves down to the foot of the hill one would think an avalanche or earth quake had visited the county by the nois they would make wen coming down, hundred of tons of stone and gravil would follow them down.

About twelve years since, I went to the Fegeei Is lands to drill a well for an English sindicate. We was not drilling for oil but for esens of peppermint which we expected to get at about 9000 feet if we failed to get a paying well at that depth we would drill to the loar sand for bay rum which we expected to get at 12000 ft. and in order to drill to so great a depth we had to have some large tools for we started the hole at 25 feet in diameter out stems was 198 feet long and 12 feet thick and other tools in the same propotion. After ariveing on the island with my tools and 16 men for we had to put eight men on tower to handle the tools, after getting the rig built the derrick being 300 feet high with 80 ft. base we got riged up and started to drill and at about 400 feet we struck some rubber rock when the drill comenced to rebound and we could not keep the tools in the hole and failure stared us in the face, but a hapy thought came to my rescue and i had the boys cut the rope of the tools and let them drop they rebounded half ways out of the hole when we grabed them and shoved them down again when the rebounding continued we keped this up for ten days when the tools finaly stoped, and after we maisured up we found we had drilled 500 ft. making our hole about 900 ft. deep at that depth was fairly good drilling we got Blue monday, hurry up sand, big lime, Coal Salt sand. all came in regular order when we cased at 3044 feet with thousand barrel iron tanks which we riveted to gather, this reduced our hole to 20 ft. in diameter and we proceeded without much trouble about 7,000 ft when we had a fishing job we broke the jars and left the tools in the hole, I went to the nearest light house on the cost and borrowed a fog horn screwed it on a sinker used it as a horn socket and fished out the tools (necesety is the mother of invention) our boiler was fired with coca nuts which make good steam but are very noisy as the explode as soon as they get hot which keeps up a continue shooting which resembles musketry, the nois did not bother us much as the boiler was over a mile away the tool dressers would ride a horse from the rig to the boiler stop on his way and take care of the pittmen.

At the depth of about 9,000 ft. we shut down one saturday to rest over Sunday we puled the tools out of the hole and hung them to one side of the derrick threw some boards over the hole and went to our boarding house to dream of a flowing well as we wer nearing that long looked for sand, but we were doomed to disappointment, on starting up on monday morning our tools stoped 200 ft. from the bottom of the well what did it mean we had no cave, we hiched on and comenced to drill we thought first we had struck some more rubber rock but shortly the tools began to go when we had let out about twenty feet of rope we pulled out and run the bailer, Christopher Columbus what a sight, one of our men cryed we have struck the jugler vain of the earth, its blood, not so fast brother I said we have struck the old devel squair in the head as you will find lots of hair mixed with the blood, and bones cryed a man to my left, and while we was examining the contents of the bailer, a nativ came into the derrick who said he was the big Noble Grand Worshipfull Master Chancler Comander Exaulted Ruler and Jibbonancy of the island, and we were murders in the eyes of their people, that we had killed all the monkeys on the island which they had held most sacred, he then solved the mistery he then told us that all the monkeys had gathered at the well on sunday to have a convention in the derrick when one of their number had axidently fell in the well when one monkey is in distress they all go to his rescue each one jumping down the hole one after the other untill they were all down the well, never to return again.